how2become

A Driving Instructor

... An Insider's Guide
by Bill Lavender

Orders: Please contact How2become Ltd, Suite 2, 50 Churchill Square Business Centre, Kings Hill, Kent ME19 4YU.

ISBN: 978-1-909229-90-7

First published 2013.

Typeset for How2become Ltd by Molly Hill, Canada.

Printed in Great Britain for How2become Ltd by Bell & Bain Ltd, 303 Burnfield Road, Thornliebank, Glasgow G46 7UQ.

VISIT MYDRIVING.CO.UK

Driving Online was established in 1996 by Bill Lavender. It was one of the first UK driving websites. The site remains independent and is designed as an information resource intended for all drivers, including readers of this book, where any necessary technical and statistical updates can be found. ADIs who subscribe to the site can download an unlimited number of the lesson plans and diagrams found in this book.

www.mydriving.co.uk continues to attract people wishing to learn to drive; it therefore supports a free ADI Directory, where provisional licence holders can find a local driving instructor by making a simple postcode search. Registration for ADIs on the site is easy, we recommend that you do this and at the same time upload a good photo of yourself in front of your training car.

CONTENTS

ABOUT BILL LAVENDER

Forward by Robin Cummins OBE
Former DSA Chief Driving Examiner

This Guide has been written by industry insider, Bill Lavender.

Well known for his "Better Training" features in adiNEWS for the last ten years, Bill became an Approved Driving Instructor in 1982 and has spent most of his career at the British School of Motoring (BSM) in various senior training and development roles, including NVQ and BTEC awards for instructors. He was also responsible for the company's learning resources, including retail products for learner drivers.

Bill now works freelance as an independent road safety consultant specialising not only in driving instructor Continuing Professional Development (CPD), but also delivering Driver Certificate of Professional Competence (dCPC) courses for professional bus and lorry drivers.

By producing this guide, Bill has reflected on his extensive knowledge and experience of the industry to provide first-hand guidance for anyone who is thinking about becoming an Approved Driving Instructor (ADI). Being a driving instructor is a very rewarding career for the right person. New learner drivers rely on good instructors who are suited to the job, to not only prepare them to pass their tests first time, but to also help them enjoy the experience of learning how to stay safe on our busy roads.

The difference between the number of people first registering with the DSA to become an ADI and the number actually qualifying is a concern. There are clearly many people who must be very disappointed for one reason or another that they have not been able to qualify or have not been able to make

a living out of the business.

It is important that every new potential instructor knows exactly what to expect from the industry and who is there to help you and the best way to ensure that all expectations are fully met.

As well as important technical information such as the lesson plans, you will find good advice on what it takes to be a successful instructor. There are many attractions to the job and how well you do really does depend very much on how you use your personality and business acumen. To this extent, Bill has included details about ways to enhance your professional CV by entering into the world of qualified driver training.

This guide will help you decide whether to go ahead with the career or not, whatever you decide, it can help you save a lot of money and time. I would recommend this guide to every single potential driving instructor.

Robin Cummins OBE

Former DSA Chief Driving Examiner

INTRODUCTION –
HOW TO BECOME A DRIVING INSTRUCTOR

Becoming a qualified driving instructor is much more than starting a new job; it is about learning the skills of a new profession. An Approved Driving Instructor's job is to teach people to drive safely and to prepare them for their driving tests. This involves not only giving instruction, but also monitoring the learner, the road and other vehicles very carefully. Learner drivers do not make deliberate mistakes. They are likely to make fewer errors where the instructor is fully in control of the learning environment by giving the correct level of tuition.

Besides an interest in driving, the starting point is having an even temperament and a personality to suit the work. Some instructors find it easier than others to be understanding, supportive and be capable of developing a good rapport with customers. Each learner driver has a different character and personality. You need to be patient – it's not always easy to be the perfect driver and spend your time sitting next to people who can't drive!

When becoming a driving instructor, it is very satisfying to consider that the skills you are teaching will provide a foundation for good driving throughout their motoring lives and also make a very valuable contribution to road safety.

It can be a long road to qualifying as an ADI, taking at least a year from making the application. Studying and preparing yourself for each part of the qualifying examination is likely to take up much of your time, it will also probably involve the support of people who are close to you. It's wise to avoid

upsetting those that you care for and respect, by not criticising mistakes in their driving, unless they do ask you for an expert opinion!

This guide hasn't been written with the intention of promoting the driving instructor career. As in other professions, those who are already qualified will say that there are already enough practitioners in their respective businesses. It is meant as an independent and impartial guide for anyone interested in finding out how to become a driving instructor.

If you have made your mind up about joining the profession, this guide is definitely for you. If you're not sure about the career, then this guide contains enough information to help you make your mind up.

CHAPTER I
WHY BECOME A DRIVING INSTRUCTOR?

WHY BECOME A DRIVING INSTRUCTOR?

Very good question. Why indeed would anyone want to become a driving instructor? Very experienced motorists may have a recollection of the original 1970s Bob Newhart sketch where the American comedian depicts a series of difficult situations occurring during a driving lesson. While Bob struggles hard to keep a grip of the lesson, his customer still enjoys it and asks to book more training! If you haven't seen the sketch, it is well worth a viewing.

Most of us in Britain will have taken a full course of professional driving lessons when we learnt to drive. Some of us would have had the advantage of private practice between lessons as well. So, we have an idea of what the work entails. No doubt we also all have opinions on driving standards and a view on how these should be improved. Each of us will probably have at least one interesting or perhaps amusing story to tell about something that happened during our training or perhaps an incident on the driving test itself. Driving is always an easy topic for discussion, even though 3.8 million out of a total 31.9 million drivers have some points on their licences; this doesn't stop us being expert drivers!

CAREER CHOICE?

You have to be at least 21 and have held a full car licence for at least four years before you can qualify with the Driving Standards Agency (DSA) as an

Approved Driving Instructor (ADI). This could be one reason that the career isn't promoted to school leavers. If you want to be a bus or lorry driving instructor then, there is less regulation. All that you will need is to have held that particular driving licence for at least three years and find a company to employ you, unless you already have your own training vehicle.

ADIs are drawn from a very wide range of different backgrounds, representing just about every industry, business and profession that you can think of. For some people, the profession can form a second income. The most common denominator is an interest in driving cars. Though the national television advertisements, attracting redundant and unemployed workers, promising high income have disappeared from our TV screens, the career still does have a vocational appeal for those who enjoy motoring and feel that they can do a good job teaching people how things should be done properly.

WHAT ARE THE ATTRACTIONS?

The majority of full-time driving instructors are self-employed. Being your own boss means not having to report to someone else, which can be a great feeling. You still need to be good with your time management; to keep your customers you will need to be reliable and punctual. In the long run, it might also be an opportunity to improve your work/life balance.

It is an advantage to manage the times that you want to work, though there can be some disadvantages, such as needing to work in the evenings or at weekends. You will need to find, or make time, to manage your financial accounts and arrange your own tax payments.

WHAT ARE THE ROLES AND RESPONSIBILITIES?

The formal responsibilities almost speak for themselves in terms of teaching "safe driving for life". As an ambassador of the road you are relied upon to set a good example in your own driving and ensuring that those you teach are kept in a safe learning environment while they gain experience behind the wheel. The roles that come into focus while teaching someone to drive can be quite varied; besides being a teacher or a coach, when you're giving advice, you're an advisor; when you're drawing diagrams, you're an artist; when you're listening you might even say that you're a counsellor or a psychologist.

CHAPTER 2
WHAT IS THE WORK LIKE?

If you enjoy driving and are a good, effective communicator, then this work can be for you. ADIs have a great deal of responsibility to teach customers the skills they need to drive safely "for life", as well as passing their driving tests.

With each new learner, you check with them about any previous driving or other relevant experience such as riding a pedal cycle or possibly a motorbike. If they have driven a car before, begin by making a practical assessment. Based on the outcome of this, you can plan a series of lessons to take the learners to the point where they can take their practical driving test.

You might also cover the theory side in more detail, although most learners will usually do this in their own time. Most driving lessons follow a similar pattern, typically covering these areas:

1. **Basic vehicle pre-driving checks.** Examples include; the importance of correct tyre pressures and regular engine component checks (various fluid levels), vehicle relevant specifications (engine size, fuel used).

2. **Car controls, equipment and components.** Examples include understanding the function of the accelerator, clutch, gears, footbrake, handbrake, steering and how to use these correctly. The benefits of ABS and electronic stability programmes.

 how2become

3. **Vehicle characteristics.** Examples include knowing the principles concerning use of speed and braking distances. This should also include road holding under various road and weather conditions.

4. **Road Procedure.** Examples include the knowledge and skills to carry out the observation routine recommended in the 'Highway Code': Mirrors – Signal – Manoeuvre (MSM); correct use of speed and position and respond promptly to all risks.

5. **Road user behaviour.** Examples include knowledge of the most common causes of collisions and which road users are most at risk and how to reduce that risk.

6. **Adapt to different driving and traffic conditions.** Examples include knowing the particular hazards in both daylight and darkness, and on different types of road.

7. **Motoring law and the 'Highway Code'.** Examples include sufficient knowledge about traffic signs, road markings, pedestrian crossing types and parking regulations.

8. **Environmental Issues.** For example, a responsible driving technique will minimise the impact on the environment as well as achieving fuel cost savings.

9. **Dealing with emergency situations.** It is important that new drivers know the action needed to avoid and correct skids, how to drive through floods and flooded areas, and what to do when involved in a collision or breakdown.

10. **Attitude.** Develop a positive attitude to all other drivers and road users. Most of their mistakes, although annoying, are made unintentionally and need to be tolerated.

For the safety of learners, yourself and other road users, you will normally teach in a car fitted with dual brake and clutch pedals. As the learner becomes more competent, you will leave the 'nursery patch' and take them on to busier roads, dual carriageways and more complex junctions, including roundabouts. Once you believe the driver has reached a high enough standard, you advise them on applying for a driving test date. To help judge this date, it is useful to conduct a Mock Driving Test that simulates the real thing. You might wish to choose an associate ADI to conduct this for you.

What skills or qualifications are needed and which of these do you already have? Good interpersonal communication skills are a must to become a successful instructor. Plenty of driving practise, preferably in different cars provides useful experience to help you instruct knowledgably and effectively.

Is the job easy? It isn't uncommon for members of the public to say to instructors "… Oh, I couldn't do your job, you must have so much patience". Your car has dual controls and you decide the route that will suit the learner, planning their learning to match their ability and develop their skills.

Learner drivers do not make deliberate mistakes. They are likely to make fewer errors where the instructor is fully in control of the learning environment by giving the correct level of tuition. The job isn't difficult providing you plan each lesson properly.

Since the DSA has actively encouraged ADIs to sit-in and watch driving tests being conducted, the number on instructors doing so has risen from around 5% to 14%. Observing driving tests is the best way to see exactly the standard that is acceptable to pass and be allowed to drive unaccompanied.

As part of the training programme, instructors can agree to manage and arrange the driving test date for their learners, as well as the preferred DSA Test Centre location. They do this to help avoid having appointment clashes, or too many tests in the same week.

When it comes to the driving test, you need to know the main driving faults. The top five ranking of these faults remains consistent, year on year:

Male – Top 5 Driving Faults	Number	Female – Top 5 Driving Faults	Number
Junctions – observation	84,343	Junctions – observation	102,706
Mirrors – direction	48,601	Mirrors – direction	58,222
Move Off – safely	39,474	Reverse Left – control	56,243
Junctions – turning right	33,865	Reverse Park – control	54,793
Response to Traffic Light Signals	30,526	Control – steering	44,246

When we examine collision statistics data for qualified drivers, we see that the pattern of mistakes continues into post-test driving, for instance, where most collisions occur at road junctions.

Finally, as in every job, there are important elements of paperwork to complete. You will need to keep an up-to-date appointment diary for customers and also a record of your business income and expenditure for taxation purposes. Keep all your payment receipts. There are companies advertised that provide various levels of administrative help and accountancy services.

CHAPTER 3

HOW TO MAKE A LIVING

Most driving instructors are self-employed and work freelance, though some work under what is called a "franchise", although it might be more accurate to describe it as a "business licence", where you're permitted to use a company name such as; AA, BSM or RED. You will have to sign a Service Level Agreement (SLA) that you will be held to in the event of any dispute. This will govern the use of any car supplied, along with the use of promotional materials and their intellectual property.

WHO ARE OUR COMPETITORS?

There are currently 46,569 Approved Driving Instructors (ADIs) on the Driving Standards Agency's Register. This figure has recently fallen after gradually rising over successive years. The majority of ADIs teach only part-time, or have gained the qualification while they were between other jobs, or because they are involved in another professional area of road safety.

WHAT IS THE MARKET?

The number of new applicants for a provisional licence has remained fairly constant though figures suggest that people might be postponing learning to drive until they have the finance.

The number of candidates taking tests over the last two years:

Year	Tests conducted
2011	1,621,000
2010	1,513,620

These figures will include re-attempts at the test. Based on driver records since 2004, the biggest number of people re-attempting the car practical test is 36 and 105 for the car theory test. The majority of L-Test candidates take some training with an ADI. DSA report that some 93% of tests are conducted in driving school cars every year.

We know from our own experience that the cost of motoring isn't just about buying a car. The associated running costs, particularly car insurance have always been considered high, especially for the new drivers aged under 25. As with anything in life, if you need something, you will need to find the money. Competing demands on the pocket of the young driver are nothing new. They have choices how they spend any disposable income. Fashion clothing, entertainment as well as keeping up with the latest must-haves has always existed. The introduction and increase in the cost of college tuition fees are a disincentive for some potential customers in this age group, but like having a full licence, this is an investment in their own future. There will always be adversities and excuses, despite these, young people will want and need to get their full driving licence, and usually as soon as possible.

The insurance cost is calculated on personal injury risk to the driver and similar expensive third party claims, rather than the cost of replacing vehicles which is normally relatively small. Where the new driver agrees to an insurance company using telematics monitoring and parental controls, this can help make this cost more affordable.

In terms of income expectations, establishing a new business will always take some time and its growth will depend on good planning and a full commitment. Some experienced instructors can turn over the advertised figure of £30,000 a year. This is however a very optimistic assumption and it can't be taken as an average.

Typical income has to be based on the cost of an hourly driving lesson and the amount of hours worked. Lessons fees range on average from around £15 to

more than £30 an hour and some instructors may be prepared to work more than 48 hours a week. Costs (eg car maintenance, fuel, franchise/licence fees, pension scheme, holiday and sick pay and other expenses) would also have to be taken out of the income.

Instructors working through a franchise, or business licence would usually pay a weekly fee that can be up to £300, but in return will be provided with a car. They would also pay for their own fuel. Some franchise agreements make an extra charge for each new customer they provide.

Whatever business model or scheme you decide to follow, the potential earnings are ultimately dependent on your popularity with customers, along with your ability to understand the business and make it work for you.

To protect your income, you will need to have an effective terms and conditions agreement with your customer. This will make the rules clear, ensuring lesson pre-payments and a lesson fee cancellation policy. You can get help and advice on this area by being a member of one of the instructor trade organisations.

CHAPTER 4
HOW TO PLAN YOUR BUSINESS

First, you need to be legal and therefore have to become fully qualified before you can operate on your own. Then the business things to consider are:

1. **The car.** Should you buy a new or second-hand car outright? Alternatively it can be more tax efficient to lease a car direct from the manufacturer, a car leasing business or an established driving school. Dual controls are essential for safety. However, they may not be fitted as part of any offer or deal.

   ADI industry magazines provide training vehicle ratings as well as informative reviews and updates. You will want to consider – fuel type and economy, servicing, warranty, roadside assistance, insurance and courtesy car costs. Check the car's reputation for build and reliability for those thousands of tuition miles; comfort for all shapes and sizes of learners, easy cockpit drill and use of gears, along with suitability for accuracy and observations when reversing.

2. **Your customers.** How will you source your learners? It will take time to establish your business and gain word of mouth recommendations, so, posting an advert in a local shop window, distributing flyers at events, advertising in the local newspaper and/or promoting yourself on social media such as Facebook, are all steps towards getting your first customers and building your reputation as a reliable and popular instructor.

3. **Driving School Franchises.** National, regional and local schools do offer franchise schemes that will offer you both a car and possible stream of new customers. These schemes, or business licences, are normally based on a formal contract agreement that will probably commit you to a long minimum term. Seriously consider taking independent advice or at least ask around before committing yourself.

    As with any financial venture, you need to do your own research before making any agreement. A good starting point is the industry's trade magazines. These carry advertisements from the various suppliers. You will also find adverts from companies aiming to support your every business need, whether it is accountancy, promotional stationery such as business cards, or personalised call answering services. You can check their websites and make contact with them.

    The internet is a great resource, but you will need to discriminate by picking out the best information. Facebook also now supports a number of driving instructor groups including some that offer excellent practical advice on business and marketing. Be selective about any online purchase you're considering.

CHAPTER 5

HOW TO MAKE THE BEST OF YOUR CUSTOMERS

You've had the enquiry, with the usual questions; How much are your lessons? What are your discounts? How many lessons will I need to pass? You've discussed your services with the prospective customer, or the person(s) paying for their lessons. You've sold the benefits and advantages of the way you teach people to drive and made the sale. Your new customer has a provisional driving licence and is very keen and ready to start.

First impressions are the most lasting, so it's particularly important to get things right. Is your car ready? Are you looking your best? What are the ground rules and how will you manage the course?

- If the first lesson was booked with a phone call, will this be their normal means of contact?

- Where is the pick-up point: home, work or somewhere else?

- When and how will you present your business terms and conditions?

- Do you expect lesson payment before starting?

- Will you always keep one lesson payment in credit to discourage cancellations?

- How well do you know what your new customer's needs are ... is the

person a complete beginner or at some other stage in the learning process?

We need to know our customers and what makes them tick. Without a regular stream of new customers, whether sourced through recommendations or other means, you won't have a business. You need to make the best of your customers and to this end, there's a lot in this publication that will help to guide you.

When customers are asked about what they want from learning to drive they are likely to say "pass my driving test". Becoming a full licence holder means independence from public transport and costly taxis, and the freedom to get around much more easily. While there's been some tendency to demonise driving and cars as something politically incorrect, in the real world, having a driving licence opens the way to improving job and career prospects for everyone.

The influence of peers can be a factor affecting the decisions they make, such as choice of instructor or the car they wish to learn in. Their parents, who may have agreed to fund some or all of their lessons have an inclination to understate both the amount of time they personally took learning to drive as well as how much it cost them to pass their tests.

Because of increasing traffic and changes to the driving test, the amount of time needed to learn the essentials is taking longer. There are no real shortcuts to a first time driving test success, what counts the most is quality time spent training and practising behind the wheel.

A natural follow-on from a successful driving test result is to take the Pass Plus course which includes motorway driving. If you promote and sell this during basic training, it will not only benefit the new driver, but will help improve your business earnings.

In summary, to make the best of your customers, give them good attention and respect. Combine this with a high standard to tuition and you will receive many personal recommendations and you can expect your business to flourish.

CHAPTER 6
HOW TO ADAPT TEACHING TO A LEARNING STYLE

Teaching may come naturally to you. By recognising and understanding learning styles, we can adapt our teaching methods and techniques to suit each individual. This will improve the speed and quality of their learning. In short, we need to get the best balance of these:

1. Eyes – keeping things visual, for instance by using diagrams or pictures

2. Ears – providing suitable explanations and using listening skills

3. Body – getting a feeling for the movement of the car

4. Hands and feet – touch, for instance, when using the car's controls

One of the most popular ways of determining someone's learning style is to use a Honey and Mumford questionnaire. Briefly, the student is presented with a series of statements to which a response of "agree" or "disagree" is necessary, for instance:

*   I have a reputation of having a no-nonsense direct style

*   I am attracted more to new unusual ideas than to practical ones

*   Most times I believe the end justifies the means

*   I quickly get bored with methodical, detailed work

- Flippant people who cannot take things seriously usually irritate me
- I usually judge other people's ideas on their practical merits
- I think that decisions based on the analysis of the information are sounder than those based on intuition
- I prefer to respond to events spontaneously, rather than plan things out in advance
- On balance I tend to talk more than I should and I need to develop my listening skills
- I prefer to do the listening than talking
- I enjoy communicating my ideas and opinions to others
- I enjoy the drama and excitement of a crisis

There are no right or wrong responses. The answers will give some indication which learning style(s) predominates:

1. Activists … like to learn by being hands-on and doing something. They have a very practical approach to learning

2. Theorists … like to learn by understanding the theory. They like facts and to analyse, drawing new information using logic and reasoning

3. Pragmatists … like to put the learning into practice in the real world by problem solving and discussing things

4. Reflectors … like to learn by observing and thinking about what happened. They prefer to stand back and view experiences from a number of different perspectives, taking time to come to an appropriate conclusion.

There are a number of academic theories about how people learn. This learning styles model is based on David Kolb's 'Experiential Learning' cycle. The benefit of looking at this is that it helps to improve the way that we deliver standard lesson content to each individual learner.

As an example, on a driving lesson where the learner is more of an 'activist' then the amount of briefing may be minimal. Most practical driving faults would be dealt with on the move. Where the learner is more of a theorist then any briefing might need to be a little longer and you should consider pulling up on the roadside more, to review relevant learning points.

CHAPTER 7

HOW LEARNERS LEARN TO DRIVE

THE LEARNING PROCESS –
THE STAGES FROM INCOMPETENCE TO COMPETENCE

If learning is properly structured with regular lessons, then it is more likely to be successful. You choose when a subject needs explanation, demonstration and the level of instruction for practise. You also determine the type and how many questions to ask and when to ask them.

Learning is best achieved when topics are taught from what is known, to what is unknown. A popular way of looking at how a learner gains skills, is the 'Conscious Competence' learning model. In brief:

1. **Unconscious incompetence.**   "I don't know what I don't know"
   The learner does not understand or know how to drive and is not aware of how much there is to learn to become a competent driver.

2. **Conscious incompetence.**   "Ahh, there's something I don't know"
   The learner recognises the skills involved to drive a car. The making of mistakes can be integral to the learning process. Plenty of encouragement needs to be given.

3. **Conscious competence.**   "I can do this when I'm deliberate about it"
   The learner understands or knows how to do something. Performing the skill requires concentration. There is significant conscious effort to execute the new skill.

4. **Unconscious competence.**   "I can do this without even thinking"
   The learner can drive competently. With enough practise the skill has
   become second nature and can be performed easily.

One example to demonstrate this competence model, when learning to drive
a manual car, is how to use the gearbox correctly. For example:

i.   At first you don't know what the gears are or how to use them.
      (Unconscious incompetence)

ii.   You find out the benefits of the gearbox and how to use the lever in
      coordination with the clutch and begin to practise, but make mistakes.
      (Conscious incompetence)

iii. With focus and concentration you make no mistakes.
      (Conscious competence)

iv.   With practise you can change gears effortlessly as though on auto-
      pilot and at the same time perform other driving tasks successfully.
      (Unconscious competence)

As the driver develops in the unconscious competence phase, there is the
potential danger of familiarity breeding contempt. For instance, in forward
planning, the new driver begins to take calculated risks such as crossing
traffic signals as they turn red. Drivers can begin to drive "on memory" rather
than "on sight". Also, as our perception of improved roads and better cars
make us feel safer then we might be liable to take more risks.

These are issues to keep in mind when adapting the lesson plans in Appendix
2 of this guide to each learner's stage of ability. There is plenty of work for the
instructor to do to ensure that learners earn their Certificate of Competence to
Drive at the first attempt. Learners who fail their test generally do so because
they are insufficiently prepared.

On average, people who pass their driving test have had 47 hours of driving
lessons with a professional instructor, along with 20 hours private practise.
The actual number of lessons needed to achieve competence will depend on
the individual learner's ability, along with the frequency and length of lessons.
Research indicates that where learners do combine professional lessons
with private practise, there is less risk of a serious collision happening after
passing the test.

CHAPTER 8
HOW TO BE A GOOD DRIVING INSTRUCTOR

Make a good first impression, begin with a smile. You are your best advertisement so make sure that you look the part. You can dress in comfortable clothing, but always take care to look smart. Keep your car in a clean and roadworthy condition, also drive it as a professional at all times. Most driving instructors would say that you need to be a people person to succeed in this line of work. They would also say that they enjoy driving and aspire to achieve a high first-time pass rate.

As instructors' personalities and characters differ, so too do their approaches to the job. A serious challenge faces all professional instructors. Car transport is a commonplace and easy activity. For the majority of people; it is also the most dangerous thing they ever do. It seems almost unbelievable that traffic collisions are the most common cause of death and serious injury in the world, particularly among young people.

The one-to-one situation for over forty hours puts the driving instructor in a key position to influence the behaviour of the next generation of drivers. Once qualified, drivers, by default, are often very defensive about their driving skills and dislike criticism. Communicating the "safe driving for life" message to new drivers is an important start to improving driving standards.

 how2become

HOW GOOD ARE INSTRUCTORS?

A requirement of being on the ADI Register is that you take a periodic assessment with the DSA. This is known in the industry as a 'Check Test' and involves a specially trained examiner observing a one-hour live driving lesson.

The assessment is graded. The original intention of the grading system was to provide a mechanism for deciding when the ADI should be supervised again. The system is viewed by instructors as a measure of how good an ADI is:

Grade 6:   Overall performance to a very high standard with no significant instructional weaknesses.

Grade 5:   A good overall standard of instruction with some minor weakness in instructional technique.

Grade 4:   A competent overall performance with some minor deficiencies in instructional technique.

Grade 3:   An inadequate performance with numerous deficiencies in instructional technique.

Grade 2:   A poor overall performance with numerous deficiencies in instructional technique.

Grade 1:   Overall standard of instruction extremely poor or dangerous with incorrect or dangerous instruction.

Currently when making the assessment, the lowest grade awarded for any of Core Competency determines the final grade awarded. The Core Competencies are fault identification; fault analysis and remedial action. These are the current statistics for ADI performance nationally:

Grade	Approved Driving Instructors
6	2,834
5	15,768
4	24,529

There are around 3,500 instructors who are ungraded. Most of these will be newly qualified ADIs that have not yet taken their first Check Test, or who have received an 'E' performance grade, meaning that the assessment was an 'Educational'.

CHAPTER 9
HOW TO TEACH DRIVING

While learning to drive has to be a serious business, it should also be an enjoyable one that can have its light-hearted moments. We have to find the right balance, which might well vary from learner to learner.

With experience, instructors develop their teaching style to suit the customer's way of learning. Some learners might expect to be instructed what to do, while others might prefer a more interactive approach where open questions are frequently used. Often a blend of the different styles to suit to the subject area works best. As a typical learner progresses through a planned course of lessons, we would expect the level of instruction to be adapted to more of a prompting or coaching style. Driving a car takes account of three areas of learning. These are:

1. **Physical skill**   How to control the car safely

2. **Thinking skill**   The ability to apply the 'Highway Code' rules correctly to traffic situations

3. **Attitude**   A commitment to a defensive driving mind-set

Driving instructors confidently perform the first two areas of learning. The challenge is to permanently influence the third area. Particularly among male drivers it is attitude that determines the new driver's risk of having a serious collision after passing the driving test.

THE EUROPEAN GOALS FOR DRIVER EDUCATION MATRIX

The 4 levels that are involved in all driving tasks	Knowledge and skill the driver has to master	Risk-increasing factors the driver must be aware of and be able to avoid	Self-evaluation
1. Mastery of vehicle manoeuvring	The physics of driving, handling when braking, cornering and accelerating	Risks connected with advanced vehicle technology. Distraction through smart phone use	Personal strengths and weaknesses with basic driving skills when manoeuvring in hazardous situations.
2. Mastery of traffic situations	General driving knowledge and skills. Applying 'Highway Code'. Observation and anticipation	Awareness of poor safety margins, neglect of rules, adverse driving or traffic conditions	Level of hazard perception, from a viewpoint of strengths and weaknesses
3. Goals and context of driving for a specific trip	Trip related considerations. Effects of goals, environment choice, effects of social pressure, evaluation of necessity	What is the purpose of the journey? What are the conditions likely to be? Any social pressures?	How well has the trip been planned? What are the goals, motives, feelings and expectations?
4. Goals for life and your skills for living	What are your life goals and values? What's your behavioural style and how does it affect your driving?	Risks connected with: social/peer pressure to perform a particular way. Lifestyle habits that create driving risk	Awareness of personal tendencies: Impulse control, motives, fatigue, stress, lifestyle and values, coping strategy

 how2become

The official standard for learning to drive is focused on the driving test requirements. To address driver attitude, some instructors chose to develop their driver training to include the European "Goals for Driver Education" (GDE) matrix. This is designed to encourage the new driver to think more of others on the road and how to avoid a high-risk driving style.

At the start of a course in learning to drive, learners begin by mastering the car's controls and then learn how to read the road ahead. These are the first two levels in the GDE Matrix. After passing the test, the human factors in the next two matrix levels come into effect. This is where drivers express their personality, attitudes and motivations through their driving. While learning, the new driver's behaviour is matched to the conditioned behaviour expected to pass the test, so most ADIs won't normally see the higher levels. Once the test is passed, the new driver has the opportunity to practise driving in a style that is more compatible with their own personality.

Linking the DSA Pass Plus syllabus, with the human factors associated with the driving task provides instructors with an opportunity to identify and discuss potentially dangerous driving styles, as they develop as a consequence of the drivers own beliefs and attitude to the driving task post-test.

Besides Pass Plus being a step forwards towards completing the practical driving experience gap. It also may provide ADIs with an opportunity to see the expressive phase and provide an opportunity to prepare the new driver for one of the advanced driving tests.

Good ADIs will utilise their coaching skills to ensure that learning takes place at a far deeper level than if the new driver was purely instructed. In recent years, the term 'coaching' has gradually moved from sport into all types of training and development. We should consider the difference between coaching and instruction and how we can effectively use both:

Instruction – this is tailored into mostly full and guided instruction. When we're dealing with a complete novice or Partly-Trained learner, we need to instruct them until they firstly gain confidence and secondly, remember what to do and when to do it. We are teaching them to learn a new skill.

Coaching – is more by suggestion or possibly demonstration than instruction. Coaching is giving the driver an idea to try out, thereby taking more ownership and responsibility for, driving better.

Coaching skills, used appropriately, will raise awareness and build self-responsibility. For instance, Pass Plus drivers, who have been coached, would be expected to understand how to take ownership of the driving task and make decisions that take account of their strengths and limitations.

CHAPTER 10

HOW TO QUALIFY AS A DSA APPROVED DRIVING INSTRUCTOR

For anyone wishing to qualify as a driving instructor, the Driving Standards Agency (DSA) is the awarding body. To become an ADI, you have to pass a three-part entry examination with the DSA. Last year, while 6,930 people began the registration process, only 3,339 candidates successfully qualified as ADIs.

You should therefore choose your training provider very carefully. There is a voluntary scheme administered by DSA that lists inspected businesses on the 'Official Register of Driving Instructor Training Establishments' (ORDIT). This list can be found at www.gov.uk website.

Any training you take should build on your driving and communication skills experience. This is likely to focus mainly on the technical skills you need to demonstrate to pass the DSA's three-part qualifying examination. DSA not only conduct the qualifying examination, they also supervise qualified driving instructors, providing a performance grade at the end of each 'Check Test'. This determines the period before the next assessment check.

It may be some time since you took any form of public examination, so you'll need someone who knows the format well and has the experience and understanding to adapt to your own learning style, and ultimately build your confidence. If you know someone who can recommend an ADI Trainer, then this is a good next step.

How will you study and best prepare for each part? How will you relate the multiple-choice questions, including hazard perception video clips to the two practical parts?

The three part ADI qualifying examination:

1. Part One – Your Knowledge. This is a computer-based theory test that includes multiple-choice questions along with a hazard perception test using video media.

2. Part Two – A driving test. This is a practical test of your own driving ability using a manual car.

3. Part Three – An instructional ability test. This is a practical test of your instructional ability where the examiner conducts your assessment using role play.

You are limited to three attempts to pass each practical test.

HOW TO PASS THE 'PART ONE'. THE PASS RATE IS 47%.

This begins with a knowledge test lasting a maximum of 90 minutes. Using a computer, you will be asked 100 questions and will have a choice of four possible answers for each one. This will be followed by a hazard perception test using a total of 14 video clips. You will need to click the mouse or tap a key on the keyboard each time you see a 'developing hazard'.

How the test is marked.

On the multiple-choice questions you have to score at least 85% overall and a minimum of 20 out of 25 in each of four question bands. These are:

1. Road Procedure

2. Car Control and Vehicle Mechanics

3. Motoring Law, Disabilities and the Driving Test

4. Publications and Instructional Techniques

On the hazard perception element the maximum score that can be achieved is 75 out of 75. To achieve this you need to anticipate every developing hazard as early as possible in each of fourteen clips. One of these clips has two developing hazards. The maximum score for each hazard is 5 and you need to score a minimum of 57 to pass. The minimum hazard perception score to pass a car theory test is 44.

To discourage learning the test questions and answers by rote, DSA no longer publish the official multiple-choice question bank. Instead, practise questions that cover the same learning points are commercially available from DSA and other publishers.

Potential instructors need up-to-date foundation knowledge, combined with an understanding of driving. The most important publications to study are:

- The 'Highway Code' (available online as a free download)
- Driving – The Essential Skills (available online as a purchase)

It is also important to be totally familiar with:

- Know Your Traffic Signs (available online as a free download)
- Your Road to Becoming an ADI, known as the ADI14 (available online as a free download)

The DSA recommend the 'Driving Instructors Handbook' by Miller & Stacey. This is a comprehensive reference book for all ADIs. If you plan to buy this, make sure that you purchase the latest edition. It can be bought online through Amazon or at good high street bookshops.

Distance learning packages are available from training organisations, though most potential instructors purchase their study materials and manage their own studies at a pace convenient to themselves.

HOW TO PASS THE 'PART TWO'. THE PASS RATE IS 51%.

This main part of this test is an assessment of your driving ability. This will last about an hour. You are expected to drive as an experienced motorist, demonstrating the best practices of road safety and not like a good learner. While the standard to pass is referred to as 'advanced', the thinking behind the assessment criteria is more in keeping with the DSA's publication 'Driving – The Essential Skills' rather than the police driver's handbook – 'Roadcraft'.

What this test includes:

1. an eyesight test
2. vehicle safety questions
3. an assessment of your driving ability

1. **The eyesight test.** You must be able to read a new-style vehicle number plate from a distance of at least **26.5** metres. Where the vehicle is fitted with an old-style plate the minimum distance is **27.5** metres.

2. **Vehicle safety questions.** The examiner will ask a total of five questions relating to basic vehicle maintenance; three will be 'show me' questions, where you'll need to show how you'd carry out the vehicle checks and there will be two 'tell me' questions where you'll need to explain how you'd carry out the vehicle checks.

   • A driving fault is recorded for each incorrect answer and a serious fault is marked if you answer all 5 questions incorrectly.

3. **Driving ability.** You'll need to provide your own vehicle and the DSA have some rules governing what types of car you can or can't use on driving tests. For instance, you can't use a convertible and it cannot be fitted with a 'space saver' tyre.

Unless you'll only be teaching in automatics, it has to be a manual car with right-hand drive. It will need to be fitted with an adjustable rear view mirror for the examiner's use and have an easily adjustable seat with a head restraint for a forward-facing front passenger. Broadly speaking the car must be legal, roadworthy and capable of normal performance for vehicles of its type.

The route will involve varying road and traffic conditions, including motorways or dual carriageways where possible. The examiner will assess your:

• expert handling of the controls

• use of correct road procedure

• anticipation of the actions of other road users and then taking appropriate action

• sound judgement of distance, speed and timing

• consideration for the convenience and safety of other road users

• ability to drive in an environmentally friendly manner

You will also be assessed on your ability to carry out all of the following manoeuvres:

• move away straight-ahead or at an angle

• overtake, meet or cross the path of other vehicles

- turn left-hand and right-hand corners

- stop the vehicle as if you're in an emergency

- drive in reverse and enter limited openings to the right and left

- reverse park the vehicle into the space behind a parked car

- reverse park into a parking bay

- turn the vehicle to face in the opposite direction using forward and reverse gears

There will be a section of independent driving. You will have to drive without turn-by-turn directions from the examiner for around 10 minutes. You'll have to follow either:

- traffic signs

- a series of directions given to you before you set off

- a combination of both

The examiner's assessment. There are three types of faults that can be marked:

1. a dangerous fault – involves actual danger to you, the examiner, the public or property

2. a serious fault – could potentially be dangerous

3. a driving fault – not potentially dangerous, but if you make the same fault throughout your test it could become a serious fault

You will pass the test if you make:

- no more than 6 driving faults

- no serious or dangerous faults

HOW TO PASS THE 'PART THREE'. THE PASS RATE IS 34%.

This is a test of your instructional technique. This will last about an hour. It is conducted by the examiner performing role play, portraying two learners at different stages of ability. The low pass rate reflects the general feeling that is the most daunting and difficult of the three parts of the examination.

The best way to approach this part is to show a positive and flexible attitude

that makes full use of all your own previous driving experience along with any new knowledge gained while studying for your 'Part One'. One of the common misconceptions is that a different set of rules applies for learners separate from reality. What is different with the test is the relatively short length of time you have to demonstrate effective instruction. For instance, any brief you give in the first phase should be precise and relevant, lasting only a short length of time. When dealing with the practical element, focus needs to be on the given scenario, looking for opportunities to develop skills, rectifying any genuine faults as you do so.

Your practical instruction needs to match the ability of the person in role. The roles are:

- a beginner or partly-trained pupil

- a pupil who is trained

- a qualified driver taking driver development training

The examiner will stay in character as the 'pupil' when the test starts and comes out of character only to help make instructions clearer and for road safety reasons.

Pre-Set Test (PST) exercises are used. These are based on the syllabus for learning to drive. You'll be asked to cover two exercises – one for each of the two roles the examiner chooses. The exercises are:

- safety precautions on entering the car and explanation of the controls

- moving off and making normal stops

- reversing the car and entering limited openings to the right or left

- turning the vehicle round in the road to face the opposite direction

- parking close to the kerb, using reverse gear

- practical instruction in how to use mirrors and make an emergency stop

- approaching and turning corners

- judgement of speed and general road positioning

- dealing with emerging at T-junctions

- dealing with all aspects of crossroads

- dealing with pedestrian crossings and giving appropriate signals

- meeting, crossing the path of and overtaking other vehicles

Your driving instruction should be tailored to the standard of the 'pupil' the examiner is playing and the time managed to the 30 minutes available for each part. You can ask the 'pupil' questions to find out more about their knowledge, but take care not to interrogate. You can also:

- use lesson plans, diagrams and training aids

- refer to notes or subject headings – but you can't read at length from notes or books

As with the briefing, keep any stationary instruction short and be prepared for the 'pupil' to ask you questions. Your instruction needs to be natural, giving your 'pupil' a chance to show you what you've taught them. Any errors should be corrected in a proactive manner.

A common failing on this test is where an attempt is made to demonstrate the full sum of knowledge on the PST. You have shown this already, by passing the first two parts of the exam. Continue to be natural, as though on a real lesson. The information you give needs to be 100% relevant to the practical scenario and the appropriate aspects prioritised. One of the secrets is to listen very carefully to the 'pen picture' presented by the examiner at the start of each phase, then be ready to use appropriately, a combination of methods, techniques and levels of instruction to ensure that learning is achieved.

Currently, the three main areas of the examiner's assessment are; core competencies, instructional techniques and instructor characteristics:

1. **Core competencies. The examiner judges how well you:**

    - identify and prioritise faults

    - analyse and explain faults

    - give instruction to correct faults

2. **Instructional techniques. The examiner judges how well you:**

    - match your level of instruction to the ability and experience of the 'pupil'

    - plan the lesson

    - control the lesson

    - communicate with the 'pupil'

    - use 'Question and Answer' technique

    - give feedback and encourage the 'pupil'

You will also be judged on when and why you use the dual controls.

3. **Instructor characteristics. The examiner assesses whether you:**

- have a relaxed and friendly manner, but aren't overly familiar

- appear confident and are able to fill your 'pupil' with confidence in a patient and tactful way

As with the ADI 'Part 2' test, you'll need to provide your own vehicle and again, the DSA have some rules governing the type of car that you can use and how it is presented. It must:

- be taxed, insured and have a valid MOT if it needs one

- be a saloon, hatchback or estate car with a rigid roof

- be in a roadworthy and clean condition

- have working seat belts

- have manual transmission

- have right-hand drive

- have an easily adjustable driving seat

- have a forward-facing front passenger seat

- have head restraints for both front seats

- have an internal rear-view mirror that the examiner can use when sitting in the driving seat

- not be fitted with any 'space saver' tyres

- display 2 L-plates or D-plates in Wales

Your test will be cancelled and you'll lose your fee if your car doesn't meet the rules.

INSURANCE POLICY

Because the examiner will be driving your car, the insurance must cover:

- the examiner's liability for all third-party and damage risks

- liability to all passengers

- any Driving Standards Agency (DSA) examiner

The DSA do not normally give out personal information for your insurance. In rare situations, on the day of the test the examiner will give you their full name and confirm they are over 25-years-old.

THE EXAMINER'S ASSESSMENT

At the end of your test, the examiner will grade your overall performance using a bi-polar sliding scale ranging from 1 to 6; where a Grade 4 is achieved on both parts of the test, you will pass. If you can achieve a Grade 5 or 6 you have exceeded the requirements. Anything below Grade 4 is sub-standard. Whatever the result, you will be offered a debriefing on your performance at the end of the test.

TAKING THE ADI EXAMINATION AND PRACTISING TEACHING

You must pass each part before taking the next. You can sit the theory test as many times as you need to, but you are limited to three attempts at the practical test within two years of passing the Part One.

Once you have passed the first two parts of the ADI exams, you can opt to join the trainee licensing scheme. This is an optional licence valid for six months, known in the industry as the 'Pink Badge'. This has to be displayed along the nearside edge of the windscreen, above the tax disc, when giving driving lessons. Although this licence is not compulsory, the teaching practice and experience should help achieve success with the Part Three test. The trainee licence is valid for six months and entitles you to receive payment for driving instruction with a driving school. This sponsorship will require you take a minimum of 40 hours compulsory training. If you are a trainee licence holder, you will need to take a further 20 hours before your first attempt at Part 3. Further elements of 5 hours will be necessary, before you re-attempt the test. The examiner will ask for written proof of the extra training at the beginning of the test.

When you have passed all three parts of the exams, you will be fully qualified and will need to apply for your registration certificate, known as the 'Green Badge' to display along the nearside edge of your windscreen, above your tax disc. You must apply to join the register within one year of passing the Part Three test. To retain your ADI Registration, you must be available to have one lesson supervised at the ADI Registrar's request. This is known as the DSA 'Check Test'.

HOW LONG WILL IT TAKE ME TO QUALIFY?

This depends on both your own learning ability and the availability of tests from the DSA. There are three tests to pass separately within a two year time limit. If you don't pass within this time you need to start again. You should not take any test until you know what is involved and have had sufficient preparation and training. The waiting period for all tests depends on the demand in your area. The DSA's CRB contractor, TMG CRB, aims to complete 90% of application checks between four to six weeks.

HOW HARD ARE THESE TESTS?

After reading the information and detail in this guide, you will have a good idea of how hard or easy, each test might be for you as an individual.

You should ensure that you take at least one mock or simulated test when you have completed each stage of your training. Act on any feedback or other advice before you take the real thing. If necessary, you should postpone your test. Do not take it for the experience of doing so.

Taking a mock Part 1 test is easy with the software that is readily available. An experienced ORDIT trainer will be able to simulate either of the practical tests for you. You might personally consider that there is some merit in taking one of the advanced driving tests, before taking your 'Part 2' test of driving ability. If you do, be mindful that the assessment criteria are based on 'Roadcraft' which has some different emphasis to "Driving – the Essential Skills".

There's probably much more to becoming a qualified driving instructor than you expected. No test is hard if you are properly prepared. Some candidates need more time to get ready, especially for the Part Three test. If you have teaching experience already, this will help. If not, then getting some teaching practice on a trainee licence will probably be a benefit for you. Discuss the option of supervised lessons with your trainer. As always, it's a matter of individual ability, getting plenty of good practice in the correct environment and making your best effort.

WHAT ARE THE COSTS INVOLVED?

You will need to pay fees to the DSA for each of the three tests and your licences. The DSA fees currently are:

Exam Part / Licence	What is it?	Cost
ADI Part One	ADI Registration. Includes CRB check and one attempt at the combined theory and hazard perception test	£ 90
ADI Part Two	A one-hour "advanced" driving test	£111
Trainee Licence	Optional six-month licence for teaching practise. 'Pink Badge'	£140
ADI Part Three	A one-hour instructional ability test	£111
ADI Licence	Full licence renewable every four years. 'Green Badge'	£300
Total DSA Fees	**With trainee licence**	**£752**
Total DSA Fees	**Without trainee licence**	**£612**

ADI TRAINING FEES

These will depend on your choice of Training Provider and will vary considerably. You need to ensure that you choose a trainer that is on the Official Register of Driving Instructor Training (ORDIT) list.

It is time well spent if you do your own research before committing yourself to any agreement. Do make full enquiries as to the cost and what happens, if you are not successful.

Some providers will charge by the lesson, which is often an hour in duration. Others may charge a block fee for the entire course, or part thereof. You need to find out who is the best within your own locality.

If the idea of becoming an ADI is for you, the next step is how to apply.

APPLYING TO BECOME A DRIVING INSTRUCTOR

To be eligible for the DSA Register of Approved Driving Instructors, you must:

1. have held a full UK or EU driving licence for at least four years out of the last six

2. have not been disqualified during the last four years

3. complete criminal record and motoring conviction checks

4. pass the two practical exams within two years of passing the theory test

Ideally, as a potential or qualified ADI you should have a clean driving licence. The Registrar may refuse an application, if you have a certain number of points on your licence depending on the circumstances.

To register as a Potential Driving Instructor (PDI) you will need to:

- **obtain an enhanced Criminal Record Bureau (CRB) disclosure.** You can do this by calling the DSA's contractor, TMGCRB on 0870 251 5000. They will ask you some questions before they either give you access to the online application form or send a disclosure application form to you by post

- **make an application to the DSA.** When you do this online, you will need to provide proof of your identity to a Crown Post Office, who will, for a counter fee, check your ID and update TMG CRB. Alternatively, you can download the application form (ADI3) from www.gov.uk. Complete it, enclose the fee and post to the DSA.

When applying, you will need:

- your driving licence number

- your criminal record disclosure number along with the date it was produced (unless you've been told not to get one yet)

- details of any motoring or non-motoring offences, and disqualifications from driving

- details of any court cases being brought against you

CHAPTER II

HOW TO GET MORE OUT OF YOUR NEW QUALIFICATION

You will have worked very hard to become an Approved Driving Instructor. To keep your knowledge up to date, as well as your personal driving and teaching skills it is worth investing some time in your own Continuing Professional Development (CPD). You need to prioritise and decide what you need to do better. Here are some ideas:

BUSINESS CPD

Once qualified, the most important professional development has to be managing your own business successfully. Teaching someone to drive has its great rewards, especially when someone that you have taught from the beginning, passes first time without any driving faults being recorded. If you don't have another customer to replace each test success, then your talents are not only being wasted, but also your business will not succeed.

A successful business must have a continuing flow of new customers. To ensure this you will need to devise and properly implement a business plan. This will include ways to attract new customers to your school as well as how to keep them.

 how2become

TECHNICAL CPD

Teaching learners regularly can have a negative impact on your own driving, so it is worthwhile considering taking one or more of the advanced driving tests with such organisations as the IAM, RoSPA or the DIA. Re-tests are also a good idea, which RoSPA include automatically for their members. The DSA also run the 'Cardington Special Driving Test' for ADIs. This is assessed at the same high level used when training new driving examiners.

The DIA offer a five-part examination known as the 'Diploma in Driving Instruction'. This is a test of knowledge covering:

1. Legal obligations and regulations

2. Management practices and procedures

3. Vehicle maintenance and mechanical principles

4. Driving theory – skills and procedures

5. Instructing – practices and procedures

A certificate is issued for each module and the Diploma is awarded when all five modules have been completed. Broadly speaking, other forms of technical CPD are divided into two types:

1. **Course attendance.** National ADI organisations such as the Motor Schools Association (MSA), the Driving Instructors Association (DIA) and the ADI Joint Council (ADINJC) run nationwide bespoke CPD courses that will be of genuine interest to most ADIs. Other courses are also available such as BTECs. These include an award in 'Driving Science' and 'Coaching for Driver Education'.

2. **Event attendance.** Road safety organisations such as the Royal Society for the Prevention of Accidents (RoSPA) and the Association of Industrial Road Safety Officers (AIRSO) organise regular events that can be of interest to ADIs. These prove to broaden the instructor's perspective beyond the training of novice drivers.

Whether you attend a course, or an event such as a conference or a seminar, the organisations hosting these will usually provide an attendance certificate that contributes towards your voluntary CPD. In line with the mandatory 'Driver Certificate of Professional Competence' (dCPC) for bus and lorry drivers, ADIs are officially being encouraged to complete and record at least 7 hours CPD annually. You may wish to have your CPD certificates available when you take your 'Check Test'.

QUALIFIED DRIVER TRAINING

The core business for most ADIs is teaching learner drivers. One way to progress your career is to vary and diversify your work.

On 6 February 1995, DSA introduced a scheme for newly qualified drivers to take further training to help reduce the risk of costly collisions. 'Pass Plus' is a voluntary scheme that is an excellent way for new instructors to start getting experience training qualified drivers as well as generating extra business income.

With the driving test out of the way, you can adapt more of a coaching approach to the development sessions. Using the DSA's 'Pass Plus' syllabus you can deal with the possibility of negative emotions such as anxiety, stress, fear, guilt, embarrassment, intimidation and frustration. Teaching new drivers to balance making progress on the road with being cautious, and ignoring passenger-peer taunts, is important to building confidence, esteem, self-belief and keeping the car under control and totally safe.

The 'Pass Plus' scheme for car drivers – some essential information

- 'Pass Plus' is mainly aimed at new drivers in the first year after passing their tests.

- Statistics show that new drivers are more likely to have a collision in the first two years after passing their test. This is because of their lack of driving experience.

- Traffic collisions are the single greatest killer of 15-24 year-olds. This age range of drivers are greatly over-represented in single-car and loss-of-control crashes, and collisions where the driver is turning across oncoming traffic.

- Every week, around 300 driving licences are revoked, where new drivers have gained six penalty points within two years of passing their driving tests. This totals to more than 15,000 every year.

- The scheme is aimed at new drivers to help them gain quality practical driving experience.

- The course can only be offered by ADIs who have registered with DSA for the scheme. The current fee for this is £37. Refill packs are charged at £29.

- The course is designed to take at least six one-hour practical sessions. However local conditions and time of year may mean that some

modules need to be given as a theory session. A theory session could be given, such as, if there is no motorway nearby. As a rule, at least five and a half out of six hours should be spent in the car

- Local authorities may offer help with the 'Pass Plus' course fees

- You set the course fees

- This post-test driver development consists of six separate modules, including an introduction to motorway driving. The six 'Pass Plus' modules are:

  1. Town Driving (Including 'Pass Plus' Induction)

  2. All Weather Driving

  3. Out of Town Driving and Rural Roads

  4. Night Driving

  5. Dual carriageway

  6. Motorway Driving

'Pass Plus' remains a relatively untapped market. When the scheme was first introduced, 12% of new drivers took up the course, now it is down to around 8%. Anecdotal feedback from newly qualified drivers taking 'Pass Plus' indicates they do find the learning benefits them, particularly the motorway driving and overall confidence building. However the possible insurance reductions are disappointing.

REFRESHER COURSES

Refresher driving lessons or courses are usually short, where the training is designed to fulfil a particular individual need. The course will normally employ key skills such as better awareness, anticipation and planning. Such skills enable a driver to read the road better and as a result will reduce wear and tear on a vehicle and reduce fuel consumption. Each course should to be structured to suit specific learning requirements such as:

1. **Nervous drivers.** For example, someone who has recently passed the test but still feels too nervous to drive alone. Your customer could be someone who has been involved in a traffic collision and is nervous about the prospect of driving again. Refresher courses for nervous drivers will need to begin in a quiet location and gradually build up

to busier and more complex traffic conditions, but only at a rate that the driver feels comfortable with. The aim will be to boost the driver's confidence, particularly in the traffic conditions they are likely to experience.

2. **Senior drivers.** With the gradually increasing number of elderly drivers on the road, some may feel they will benefit from refresher training. As a driver must legally renew their licence at the age of 70, plus every 3 years after this, it is the driver themselves who determines whether they are fit to drive. Refresher driving lessons for the elderly offer the driver increased confidence in their abilities by eliminating bad habits and increasing hazard awareness. Such courses are not intended to prevent or discourage elderly drivers from staying behind the wheel.

3. **Non UK residents.** An overseas licence holder may legitimately drive in the UK for up to twelve months on their full licence. One of the dilemmas visitors to Britain face is if they intend on driving, they will not be familiar to driving on the left. The majority of countries drive on the right, so driving on the other side of the road is likely to be a daunting without a little professional tuition. The high frequency in which roundabouts are used in the UK can also pose an issue to many who may only come across them rarely.

4. **New UK residents.** The UK has a driving licence exchange agreement with 50 other countries. 32 of the approved countries drive on the right. Since 1997 over 1.1 million foreign drivers have exchanged their own licences for a UK one; in 2011 some 83,533 licences were exchanged compared with 30,737 fifteen years ago, suggesting that this is growing market. Training should build on their previous driving experience and be tailored to the 'Highway Code'.

5. **Drivers needing to take an Extended Driving Test.** Where a qualified driver is disqualified for certain serious driving offences, a court can order that once the disqualification period has ended, that the individual must return to provisional driving licence status. To gain regain a full licence the driver must go through the entire driving test process as a learner driver does. This also includes taking the theory test.

The extended driving test is more challenging than the ordinary learner drivers test. It isn't necessarily harder, it simply lasts twice as long and involves doing more; therefore, there is a higher possibility of something going wrong.

Customers need to be prepared to complete all the manoeuvres that include reversing, that is the corner reverse; turn in the road; reverse and bay parking, as well as the emergency stop. There are currently some 5,000 extended tests carried out every year and the pass rate is over 15% higher than the learner car test which is 45.7%.

Training will need to begin with an assessment and should then progress as with any other refresher course. Candidates will expect to be given an analysis of their ability, along with an estimate of how many further lessons/ sessions are required.

DISABLED DRIVERS

Within the terms of the Disability and Equality Act 2010, ADIs may be legally obliged to provide training to someone with impairment. Teaching disabled people to drive can be exceptionally rewarding. Gaining a full driving licence often helps a disabled driver to gain more freedom and independence. You can be assured that they will work very hard to accomplish this goal.

There are some excellent courses available for ADIs who wish to specialise in this area. You can expect to cover such areas as:

- The various types of disabilities & physical conditions.
- Teaching techniques for people with physical disabilities, learning difficulties, hearing impairment.
- Knowledge on medical conditions.
- The effects of cognitive impairments.
- Older drivers.
- Driving various adapted vehicles.
- Vehicle conversion specialists.
- Wheelchair seating, loading, management & stowage.
- Visual problems and testing vision.
- Aspects of modifications, licences, insurance & driving test.

A list of Mobility Centres, including the Queen Elizabeth Foundation (QEF) is given in 'Driving – The Essential Skills'.

TOWING TRAILERS

From 1 January 1997, the permitted weights for cars drawing trailers, including caravans were reduced. Drivers qualifying after this date have needed to pass a B+E category driving test to drive tow heavier loads. From 19 January 2013 further weight restrictions will be implemented. The towing test is based on the LGV driving test.

ADI regulations do not cover B+E training; however, any accompanying driver must have B+E on their licences and have held that category for at least 3 years. A suitable vehicle and trailer, along with the facilities will also be needed to offer training for this licence upgrade.

ADVANCED AND CORPORATE DRIVER TRAINING

With around 32 million full licence holders in the UK, opportunities do exist in the qualified driver training sector. There are now legal obligations for employers to ensure that employees driving for work have their driving checked; there are also driver offender retraining schemes and speed awareness courses. Some of this work is classroom based, but may also have on-road practical elements. There are specialist training courses for drivers of all terrain 4x4 vehicles; high performance cars including racetrack experience and anti-hijacking techniques. Consider also Patient Transport Services (PTS) for drivers of NHS or private ambulance services.

Approved Driving Instructors delivering, or wishing to deliver any type of qualified driver training should consider becoming 'DSA Fleet' qualified. The qualification is not mandatory, but some Service Providers offering this type of work can insist on the certificate.

As an individual ADI, there are many organisations that you can canvas for fleet work beginning with local companies; schools; colleges; health authorities along with voluntary groups such as the Rotary and Lions Clubs. Again, think about becoming fleet registered to gain a professional advantage.

There are a number of national companies, such as the AA who own the BSM, the IAM and RoSPA , who offer corporate driver training and development. Competition amongst experienced ADIs to get this work can be quite tough. You will most certainly need to produce a professional CV that reflects all your talents, skills and abilities.

BECOMING FLEET QUALIFIED

As part of the Government's Road Safety Strategy, DSA have for the last ten years run a separate voluntary 'Fleet' register of ADIs who specialise in the training and development of company car drivers. The work is described in different ways, such as "occupational road risk", "corporate driver improvement" or "collision risk management".

The business potential for Fleet ADIs is as big as there are companies with drivers working for them. The key to business success is being able to access this market.

Slightly over 5% of the qualified instructors have chosen to take the additional qualification to become 'DSA Fleet Registered'.

There are two routes to becoming a Fleet Trainer. To prepare and qualify for this kind of work most instructors take an accredited fleet course with one of DSA's approved providers. There are about twenty of these located around the UK. The alternative is to take the three-part entrance examination administered by the DSA. The format of this exam is very similar to the ADI qualifying process.

In both instances there are fees to pay. If you take the fleet course route you will need to pay the provider's fee along with the DSA registration fee. If you take the examination route you will need to pay for each test, along with the DSA registration fee.

Further details about taking the accredited course or examination route are given in the DSA publication 'Your Guide to the Fleet Driver Trainers Register'. This can be found and downloaded as a PDF document from www.gov.uk.

You can make a postcode search to locate the nearest provider. Make sure that the course provided suits all your requirements and needs, as well as budget, before you make any commitment.

Questions to consider are:

1. How long is the course?
2. How much time is spent on classroom and in-car training?
3. How many delegates will be participating?
4. How much pre-course theoretical preparation and study is there?
5. How will the course prepare you for the real world of corporate and other qualified driver training?

During the course, you should expect to learn about the fleet market and how you see yourself fitting into it; how best to present yourself and your product as well as how to assess and identify training needs (ITN); coach and give feedback to qualified drivers. The course should cover other important areas such as, meeting clients, selling the benefits of your programme, checking driving licences, conducting vehicle safety checks, delivering a short occupational road risk presentation, developing commentary and demonstration driving techniques.

'ROADCRAFT'

The essential source of reference for the delivery of advanced driving is the 1994 (or later) edition of 'Roadcraft – the Police Driver's Handbook'. The training and development you deliver will need to be predominately in a coaching style and should be based on the advice given in this publication.

As ADIs we treat 'Driving – The Essential Skills' as the official interpretation of the 'Highway Code'. It's worth considering that, 'Roadcraft' pre-dates this considerably. Published in 1954 under the title 'Attention All Drivers' 'Roadcraft' was the first major driving technique publication in the UK, following the 'Highway Code' (1931). 'Driving – The Ministry of Transport Manual' was not published until 1969.

The same team that published 'Roadcraft' produced an excellent publication for corporate drivers titled 'Fleetcraft: The Essential Occupational Driver's Handbook'. As well as dealing with the technical aspects of driving, it addresses company obligations under health and safety law in a simple and concise way. Presently out of print and expected to remain so until 2014.

HACKNEY CARRIAGE & PRIVATE HIRE TAXIS

As an ADI you are licenced to provide driver training for both Hackney Carriage and Private Hire taxi drivers. Requirements for taxi and private hire drivers to acquire or renew their licence vary considerably amongst the 400 plus licensing authorities within the UK.

In general, the other skills, specific to taxi drivers, that you would need to teach, include a reversing manoeuvre, along with knowledge of where not to stop that could be dangerous for a passenger to alight the taxi. Drivers will need to be prepared for a few verbal questions on the 'Highway Code' as

well be able to identify some traffic signs and road markings. For wheelchair enhanced vehicles the driver will need to demonstrate correct use of the equipment.

Candidates taking a "black cab" style test will need to answer some related 'cabology' questions. Examples of these include the dimensions of the taxi, its correct tyre pressures and knowledge of what to do if a passenger leaves property behind.

EMERGENCY RESPONSE

While there is no formal requirement for people driving emergency response vehicles to be trained beyond an ordinary driving licence, the emergency services do take on a professional responsibility to provide this.

Emergency response driver training is delivered in-house or may be outsourced. Instructors delivering this training, typically come from the ranks of each service. In the instance of the ambulance service, the awarding body, Edexcel sets the standard of driver training through the IHCD (Institute of Health Care and Development) award for ambulance drivers and their instructors.

CHAPTER 12

HOW TO BECOME A BUS OR LORRY DRIVING INSTRUCTOR

You need to be aged 21 or over and have held a full, unrestricted driving licence for at least 3 years in the category in which you wish to instruct.

Becoming an LGV or PCV instructor means that you will be preparing fully qualified drivers for a professional qualification. You will also be in charge of a far larger and heavier vehicle. The maximum weight for an LGV on UK roads is 44 tonnes and the typical double-decker bus can weigh around 14 tonnes, compared to a modest driving school car that will weigh little more than one tonne.

Lorry drivers usually qualify professionally by taking a practical intensive course with a specialist driving school. While it is possible to become a bus driver in the same way, most drivers gain this vocational licence by becoming employees of one of the many companies operating service buses.

Bus instructors who complete the NVQ (Level 3) in Driving Instruction can apply to be listed on the National Register of Professional PCV Driver Trainers which is administered by People 1st, formerly GoSkills. This NVQ has many similarities with the syllabus for becoming an ADI and is gained through a process of evidence gathering to prove competence.

A voluntary registration scheme for lorry instructors was set up in 1997.

Qualification for the LGV register involves a three-part entrance DSA examination. Upon successful completion of all three parts, the instructor receives a certificate and contact details are entered onto this register.

To become an LGV instructor, you must be competent at the planning, preparing and the presentation of driver training that is suited to lorries. The same instructional techniques and methods used by an ADI will need to be not only adapted to the much larger and heavier vehicle, but also tailored to a person that already holds at least a full car licence. Training routes need to be designed that are appropriate for the category of LGV being used. Also, a suitable area of land, for the manoeuvring exercise will be needed.

The standard of the instructor's personal driving needs to be beyond reproach. This should be combined with an ability to demonstrate best practice, together with a running commentary. Report writing is also an important skill for all professional vocational instructors.

Qualifying for the voluntary LGV register is very similar to the ADI for cars. The difference for the driving ability test is that it will last about 90 minutes and includes an off road reversing exercise. Where the LGV has a trailer, there will also be an uncoupling and recoupling exercise. For the instructional ability test, role play is used and the examiner begins by explaining which of the nine possible pre-set exercises will be used. This could include someone who has previously failed an LGV test and needs extra training. The examiner will drive the vehicle and simulate faults; you will need to make sure that your instruction matches the standard and ability of the 'pupil' within the time available. As on the ADI test, you will need to observe and correct any driving errors and give your 'pupil' a chance to show what has been learnt.

THE DRIVER CERTIFICATE OF PROFESSIONAL COMPETENCE (dCPC) QUALIFICATION

LGV and PCV licence holders who are working professionally must complete dCPC to gain their Driver Qualification Card. Existing professional PCV drivers must gain their dCPC by completing 35 hours training before 10 September 2013 and the deadline for current LGV drivers is 10 September 2014. After this date, to maintain dCPC, drivers will be expected to continue attending periodic training of 7 hours per year, to continue driving professionally.

New bus, coach and lorry drivers complete the initial four part dCPC while they are training. The first part is a theory test (multiple-choice and hazard

perception), the second part is also a computer-based exercise involving case studies relating to the working life of a professional driver. The third part is a practical test of driving ability and part four is a practical vehicle safety demonstration.

dCPC has created additional training opportunities not only for driving instructors, but also other road safety professionals with the relevant background and experience. The approved courses are designed to improve road safety by developing the professional driver's skills and knowledge in such areas as:

- eco-safe and fuel efficient driving

- defensive driving techniques

- loading a vehicle safely

- health and safety, risk awareness on the road

- driving regulations, complying with relevant rules such as 'driver's hours'

- workplace equality and diversity

- disabilities and impairments

- first aid

DRIVER TRAINING IN THE COMMERCIAL AND PASSENGER TRANSPORT SECTOR

Bus and lorry companies regulate themselves with support from quangos (quasi-autonomous non-governmental organisations):

1. People 1st (PCV/Hospitality/Travel/Tourism)

2. Skills for Logistics (LGV/HGV)

Any person giving paid practical driving instruction to drive a Licence Category B vehicle (a car) must be qualified as an Approved Driving Instructor (ADI). This is not mandatory for anyone looking to provide driver training on lorries or buses in the commercial and passenger transport sector. A visit to the People 1st and Skills for Logistics websites will provide more information about working in the commercial and passenger transport sectors, along with possible career opportunities.

MINIBUSES

Drivers who gained their full licence after 1 January 1997 are only allowed to drive vehicles with up to eight seats. Because a separate D1 category test is required to drive vehicles with between eight and seventeen seats, training for this type of vehicle, particularly for school teachers is on the increase. In addition to having held this, or a PCV licence for at least three years, minibus instructors are encouraged to join MiDAS (Minibus Driver Assessment Scheme).

CHAPTER 13

HOW TO BECOME A MOTORCYCLE RIDING INSTRUCTOR

There are 5 million full motorcycle licence holders, but about 4/5ths are inactive riders. Of all life's experiences, there's little to rival the raw excitement and sensation of power when riding a bike. Whatever your choice of machine, the experience of fresh air and freedom of the open road is exhilarating, so becoming a motorcycle instructor could be an enjoyable and rewarding opportunity.

The potential instructor needs to have excellent practical riding skills, with experience preferably on a variety of machines, as a basis for giving sound instruction. The instructor will be expected to stress the necessity of protective body clothing, not just helmets, visors and gloves. Instruction then continues onto the importance of a good seat posture; using each control correctly to change speed and turn safely. On the public road, positive riding skills for road positioning are paramount. Instructors must be capable of being in control of small groups of riders using radio control, This involves managing your own personal safety as well as those you are responsible for.

To undertake DSA Motorcycle Instructor training you must have held a full motorcycle licence for at least 3 years. Furthermore, you must be at least 24-years-old, following the 3rd European Driving Licence Directive, which came into force on 19 January 2013.

You must also be "a fit and proper person" to be accepted onto the DSA register. As with potential car instructors, DSA will check if you have any unspent criminal convictions, any penalty points on your licence, been disqualified from driving/riding or have nay court proceedings pending against you.

There are four grades of motorcycle instructor, an application for each of these needs to be made to the DSA:

1. **Down-Trained CBT Instructor:** You will need to contact a local motorcycle Approved Training Body (ATB) about taking a course. Successful completion of the course will enable you to deliver Compulsory Basic Training (CBT) to learner riders signed up with that ATB.

2. **DSA Assessed CBT Instructor:** This course builds on all the initial skills taught for the Down-Trained Instructor Course and introduces the skills required to supervise CBT instructors. Successful instructors will be able to deliver the CBTs, supervise down-trained instructors and also deliver 125cc on-road training. Course completion entails a two-day DSA Cardington assessment. This run at the DSA's training and development centre at Cardington, near Bedford.

3. **Direct Access Scheme (DAS) Instructor:** For instructors wishing to teach Direct Access Scheme students on "big bikes", machines around 500cc. For this assessment role play is used where you are expected to demonstrate how to address poor techniques and teach correct control and good practice. Successful attendance for the half-day trainer assessment at Cardington will enable instructors to deliver the training for DAS in adddition to CBT.

4. **Post-Test Motorcycle Trainer:** This is the voluntary scheme for instructors who wish to train full motorcycle licence holders, known as Register of Post-test Motorcycle Trainers (RPMT).

There are two parts to the Cardington assessment (instructional and supervisory). The assessment involves role play, where the assessor portrays the part of a learner rider. On each exercise, the potential instructor needs to achieve a Grade 4 (excellent) or Grade 3 (satisfactory). A Grade 2 is unsatisfactory and a Grade 1 is poor. Scoring a 2 more than once or twice is likely to result in a fail, scoring a 1 at any stage is an automatic fail, so candidates should aim to score threes and fours. Failing either part of the assessment would result in failing the whole assessment. A down-trained instructor who fails the instructional part would also have their down-trained

certificate revoked.

The assessment is funded through charging ATBs for CBT certificates. A maximum of two attempts at the assessment can be made before being time-barred for 12 months following the second unsuccessful attempt. The two-day Cardington Assessment is likely to be a daunting and stressful experience for those not properly prepared. The DSA are very keen to stress that Cardington assessment is just that and is not a training course.

Once fully qualified as an instructor, you will be able to manage or run your own motorcycle training school, should you so wish. As in any business, the costs will be numerous and varied. As a minimum, you have to consider the purchase or lease of machines; their safe storage and maintenance; use of a piece of land that is suitable as an area to deliver on-site CBT. Instructors will be expected to commit to working at weekends and the work is subject to possible seasonal variations.

Training to become a motorcycle instructor, as with the car ADI, requires full preparation and total commitment. Becoming a motorcycle instructor is much more than taking instructor training with a local Approved Training Body (ATB), or passing the assessments with the DSA. The attributes of a motorcycle instructor tend to be that they combine a certain passion, flair and enthusiasm with a great dedication for riding and everything associated with it.

APPENDIX I
BETTER DRIVING – THE 'SMITH SYSTEM'

Since the police began keeping records of traffic collisions in 1926, their investigations have always focused on what caused the crash, with most collisions being attributed to driver error rather than a mechanical fault.

In the 1950s, three American researchers took a different approach by looking at how good drivers avoided collisions. From this work they devised a visual search method that took the form of 'five seeing habits'.

The three researchers were Harold A. Smith, John J. Cummings and Reuel A. Sherman. Smith was a professional driving instructor who worked for the Ford Motor Company in its fleet driving division, Cummings was a traffic collision investigator and Sherman was a recognised authority on occupational vision.

The concept behind the Smith System is principally one of having a 'space cushion'. This can easily be achieved by driving at an appropriate speed for the road and traffic conditions, that is, by being able to stop well within the distance seen to be clear. Having better vision ahead is a good habit that buys time to think everything out in advance. The outcome will be a defensive driving style that is smooth, progressive, unobtrusive and above all, safe. Who could want anything more?

FIVE SEEING HABITS

1. **Look well ahead**
   Aim high to steer – search 20-30 seconds ahead not just down at the vehicle in front.

2. **Spot the problems**
   Get the big picture – look out for all other hazards such as car doors opening, pedestrians stepping out from between parked vehicles. Expect the unexpected.

3. **Move your eyes**
   Keep your eyes moving – use your mirrors, avoid the fixed stare and use your peripheral vision.

4. **Keep space**
   Apply your separation distance and have an escape route – anticipate an emergency situation developing.

5. **Be seen**
   Make sure other road users see you – using eye contact, direction/brake lights, headlight signals or the horn.

For driving instructors, the Smith System is one of the effective ways to teach awareness and planning. In this lesson planning section of this guide we suggest some coaching exercises to facilitate this.

APPENDIX 2
LESSON PLANS AND DIAGRAMS

DRIVING LESSON PLANS

Failing to plan is planning to fail. The minimum lesson plan is to agree with each learner what needs to be achieved during the period of training. Then at the end of the session, an evaluation needs to be made of how much was accomplished and what needs to be done next.

LESSON STRUCTURE

Driving lessons must be planned so that you teach from the 'known to the unknown' and the 'simple to the complex'. Every driving lesson needs to have a start, a middle and an end. The usual structure includes:

- Recap at start. Concise accurate summary of the previous lesson.

- Aims & Objectives. Setting realistic and attainable targets.

- Level of Instruction. Dialogue and technique varied to suit learner's knowledge, experience and competence.

- Planning. Organised method and sequence of tuition. Time management.

- Control of lesson. Anticipate and protect the learner from danger.

- Communication. Clear and simple instructional terminology and explanations.

- Question & Answer Technique. Relevant questions, correctly timed.

- Feedback & Encouragement. Best response to learner's performance and achievements.

- Instructor's Use of Controls. Learners must always be made aware of why the instructor has used the dual controls or any of the other car's controls.

- Recap at end. Concise accurate summary of the lessons learning points.

LESSON PLAN PRESENTATION

We begin each plan with an outline of the key learning points. These map the important subject areas for the lesson. From this starting point we go into greater detail about the lesson's content, particularly in respect to delivering the lesson. The sequence we have put this in is:

1. Identify learner's stage of ability

2. Recap briefly on any relevant previous training

3. Determine what will be the core of the lesson

4. Useful hints for delivering the lesson

5. How best to say what you want to say – The phraseology

6. How we see the skill being developed

7. To assist your instructional method, we devised some easy questions to ask

8. List of typical faults to expect

SKILLS DEVELOPMENT

To help ensure that learning is achieved during lessons, we focus on skills development. To do this effectively, we need to match our instructional

method with the customer's learning style. To get the balance correct, you need find and ask the right questions in the most suitable way. We've made a résumé of the possible driving faults to expect. You should be prepared to offer fault analysis as well as remedies.

Driving skills should be introduced in a logical order that suits the learner's ability, the geographic location, the time of day when a lesson is taken, along with the prevailing road, traffic and weather conditions.

USE THESE LESSON PLANS AND DIAGRAMS ON AN ADI PART THREE TEST

These lesson plans and diagrams may be used on your ADI Part Three test. You can and should also use illustrations from other publications such as the 'Highway Code' and 'Driving – The Essential Skills' wherever you feel these are appropriate.

You can select the topic areas from each Pre-Set Test (PST) from the subjects included in this guide. We have also included topics such as 'Approaching Roundabouts' and 'Know Your Traffic Signs, Lights and Road Markings' although these are not specifically tested during the examination.

Always try to be flexible in your approach and natural in your presentation and delivery of the lesson content.

LESSON PLAN INDEX

A. Lessons for the learner driver

i.   Explanation of the Controls

ii.   Moving Away and Making Normal Stops

iii.   Use of Mirrors

iv.   Use of Signals

v.   Emergency Stop

vi.   Approaching Junctions – Major to Minor

vii.   Approaching Junctions – Minor to Major

viii.   Crossroads

ix.   Approaching Roundabouts

x.   Pedestrian Crossings

xi.   Awareness and Anticipation

xii.   Judgement when Meeting & Crossing Approaching Traffic; Overtaking; Clearances & Following Distances

xiii.   Use of Speed, Making Progress and Road Positioning

xiv.   Know Your Traffic Signs, Lights and Road Markings

xv.   Independent Driving

xvi.   Reversing into an opening on the left

xvii.   Reversing into an opening on the right

xviii. Reverse Parking

xix.   Bay Parking

xx.   Turn in the Road

You should use your own professional judgement to decide the order in which you teach these subjects and topics. Always take into account your learner's ability as well as local circumstances. A reasonable degree of proficiency driving forwards is needed before attempting to teach manoeuvres that include reversing. Begin teaching the simpler things before moving on to those that are more complex.

B. Sessions for the new qualified driver.

The 'Pass Plus' Course

i.   Town Driving

ii.   All Weather Driving

iii. Out of Town Driving and Rural Roads

iv.   Night Driving

v.   Dual Carriageway Driving

vi.   Motorway Driving

C. Sessions for the experienced qualified driver

- The Advanced Driving Course
- Corporate Driver Development

You can adapt the advanced and corporate session plans to suit other courses for experienced qualified drivers, such as the Driver Offender Retraining Schemes and Specialist Vehicle Type Training. Training providers will probably have their own course syllabus and guidance notes.

LESSON DIAGRAMS

A picture speaks a thousand words. Pre-drawn or self-drawn illustrations will make both teaching and learning easier. We have placed some diagrams alongside the relevant lesson content. You might also wish to use other excellent illustrations such as those in the 'Highway Code' and publications such as 'Driving – The Essential Skills' or for advanced/corporate driver training – 'Roadcraft'.

LESSON I: EXPLANATION OF THE CONTROLS

Including the safety precautions on entering the car (Cockpit Drill).

KEY LEARNING POINTS

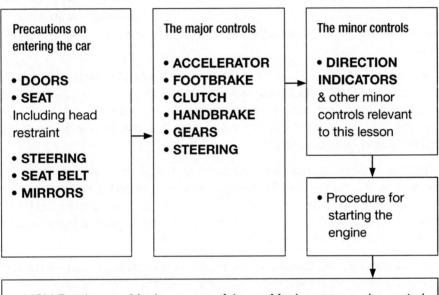

Precautions on entering the car	The major controls	The minor controls
• **DOORS** • **SEAT** Including head restraint • **STEERING** • **SEAT BELT** • **MIRRORS**	• **ACCELERATOR** • **FOOTBRAKE** • **CLUTCH** • **HANDBRAKE** • **GEARS** • **STEERING**	• **DIRECTION INDICATORS** & other minor controls relevant to this lesson

• Procedure for starting the engine

• MSM Routine   • Moving away safely   • Moving away under control
• Stopping normally in a safe position with proper use of the controls

A learner's very first lesson will normally be booked over the phone. Consider how you will introduce yourself and gain agreement about what needs to be taught, as well as how this needs to be done. It would be wrong to try and recite a script for this controls lesson. Adapt the guidance that follows to suit the learner and how he or she responds on the day.

The amount of time spent teaching the controls does depend on any previous experience or knowledge the learner has. You may need to repeat and integrate this information within the next lesson topic – Moving off and stopping.

> **Professional tip:** Use words to explain and avoid physical contact. Demonstrate using the controls and equipment on your side of the car where appropriate.

Your own driving: You are likely to need to drive your learner to a suitable area where you can introduce the car and its controls. Use this opportunity to show your learner what you will shortly be teaching. When you swap seats, out of preference, walk round the rear of the car, keeping the ignition key with you.

Core of lesson: Before beginning the controls lesson, briefly cover the daily maintenance checks to be carried out .... fuel; oil; water; lights, including indicators; tyres and that the handbrake is applied (and the gear lever is in neutral). Next, teach each learner the cockpit drill, that is, how to reach the controls safely and comfortably.

Probably the most popular cockpit drill taught by ADIs is "DSSSM" (pronounced D treble S M). There are others, but this one is particularly easy to remember. The routine is a simple version of the one published in the DSA's "'Driving – Essential Skills'. It deals with every driver's legal responsibility to sit in a position to be in full control when driving the car.

Instruction method: Questions used must be appropriate to the learner and the circumstances of the lesson. Judge the balance of 'telling' and 'Q&A' on how the learner responds to your guidance. Do keep the learner involved by encouraging safe use of the controls while the car is stationary.

EXAMPLE QUESTIONS

Cockpit drill. When you sit in the passenger seat of a car, what is the safety routine? Okay, as a driver, try this one:

- Doors. Is your door closed?

- Seat. Is your seat in a practical position?

- Steering. Can you run your hands round the whole steering wheel?

- Seat belt. Show me how you put your seat belt on

- Mirrors. What can you see in the mirrors?

Typical faults to expect during the cockpit drill

- Not closing the door properly

- Not checking in the offside door mirror or over the shoulder before opening the door

- Not checking that the door is closed

- Not asking any passengers if their doors are closed

- Not adjusting the seat position properly

- Sitting too close/far from the steering wheel

- Twisting the seat belt

- Not setting the mirrors accurately

- Moving the head when setting the interior mirror

- Touching the glass when adjusting the interior mirror

Before beginning to explain the car's controls, complete your instructor's cockpit drill to ensure that you are sat in a position to observe the learner, along with the road ahead, side and rear.

THE "CONTROLS LESSON" – FIVE AREAS OF CONTROL

1. Foot controls

2. Hand controls

3. Ancillary controls

4. Visual controls

5. Dual controls

For each control you will need to deal with:

- what it is called

- where it is located

- how to use it

- what it does

- the instructions you will give for its use.

TEACHING THE CONTROLS – IT'S AS EASY AS ABC!

Begin with the **foot controls**...

Accelerator – the 'Gas' pedal

- Located – on the right

- How to use – lightly and delicately

- What it does – increases engine speed

- Instructions – "Set gas"; "A little more gas"; "Less gas"; "Off gas"

More information – because modern cars produce significant engine torque at low RPM, the amount of gas that needs to be set is very small. Compare this to the width of a one pound coin.

Bootbrake – the **B**rake pedal

- Located – in the centre

- How to use – gently and progressively

- What it does – slows and stops the car

- Instructions – "Cover brake"; "Gently brake"; "Gently brake to stop"; "Firmly brake".

More information – include any extra detail that you consider necessary such as how the brake works on all four wheels and that three brake lights illuminate at the back of the car.

Clutch – the Clutch pedal

- Located – on the left
- How to use – slowly
- What it does – engages and disengages drive
- Instructions – "Cover clutch"; "Clutch down"; "Slowly clutch up"

Go on to the **hand controls**...

The handbrake (parking brake)

- Location – behind the gear lever
- How to use – with the button in
- What it does – secures the car
- Instructions – "Prepare handbrake"; "Release handbrake"; "Apply handbrake"; "Secure the car"

The gear lever

Located – immediately left of driver

- How to use – smoothly with palm
- What it does – enables engine power to be used efficiently
- Instructions – "Left hand on gear lever..."; "Palm towards me and select first and then second gear"; "Palm towards the front and select third and then fourth gear"; "Palm towards you and select fifth gear" Depending on vehicle, adapt instruction for selecting reverse gear eg "Lift collar, palm towards me and select reverse"

The steering wheel

Location – in front of the driver

- How to use – "pull-push" system
- What it does – changes car's direction
- Instructions – "Steer left"; "Steer right"; "Straighten the steering up".

 how2become

More information – include any extra detail that you consider necessary such as how you will teach the coordination of the foot and hand controls with forward/rear vision and use of the signals/remaining controls.

EXAMPLE OF GENERAL QUESTIONS

The controls. These questions need to be devised so that they cover what each control is called, where it is located, how it should be operated, what it does and the instructions you will give for its use.

Introduction	How familiar are you with the car's controls?

Foot controls

Accelerator	Do you know what the pedal on the right is for and how it should be used?
Brake	Do you know what the pedal in the middle is for and how it should be used?
Clutch	Do you know what the pedal on the left is for and how it should be used?

Hand Controls

Parking brake	Do you know how to use the handbrake and when it should be applied?
Steering wheel	Do you know the best position to keep your hands on the steering wheel and the recommended way to turn it?
Gear lever	Do you know what the gears are for?

Remaining controls (including ancillary controls)

Ignition key and switch (steering lock)	How do you switch the engine on?
Indicators	Do you know where the indicator stalk is and which way to use it to signal left or right?

Visual controls

Mirrors and windows
(blindspots)

Do you know where the blindspots are?

What type of glass is the interior mirror?

What type of glass are the exterior mirrors?

How will you keep the windows clean and clear?

Use 'Driving – Essential Skills' and the manufacturer's handbook to support the information you provide.

Typical faults to expect during the controls lesson

- Not positioning the right foot correctly for use between the accelerator and the footbrake
- Being heavy footed
- Not pressing the clutch pedal down sufficiently
- Not running both hands fully round the steering wheel
- Not using the ratchet button when applying the handbrake
- Not 'palming' the gear lever for correct selection during dry run
- Forcing the gear selection
- Hurrying the gear selection
- Not being aware of the blind spots
- Not being aware of the difference between flat and convex glass
- Not releasing the steering lock when attempting to turn the ignition on
- Being heavy handed with the ancillary controls.

SKILLS DEVELOPMENT

Use of the Clutch

Correct use of the clutch is essential to safe and confident car control. You will normally need to use a clear, simple diagram when explaining how it works. Depending on how quickly your learner can pick up the skill, you may need to repeat your instruction frequently. Learning to master the clutch for moving away under control and making smooth gear changes are skills that need to be constantly practised. 'Clutch control' is the skill of moving the car very slowly in first or reverse gear by fractional movements of the clutch combined with a steady gas setting. This is not the same as 'controlling the clutch' which is the skill required for moving away normally, changing gear and stopping.

Instruction method: Practise makes perfect. To assist practise, below are some examples of questions that you might ask your learner. With experience you can devise your own bank of possible questions. Questions used must be appropriate to the learner and the circumstances of the lesson. Judge the balance of 'telling' and 'Q&A' on how the learner responds to your guidance.

EXAMPLE CLUTCH QUESTIONS

Introduction	Have you seen this diagram before?
What the clutch does	Do you know what the clutch does?
When to use the clutch	When will you need to use the clutch?
How to use the clutch	Do you know how the clutch pedal should be used?
Biting point	How will you be able to tell that you have brought the pedal up far enough?
Clutch control	How will you be able to move, slow and stop the car at very low speed on a flat road or uphill?
Coordination	How should you co-ordinate the clutch with either the accelerator, footbrake and/or gear selection?

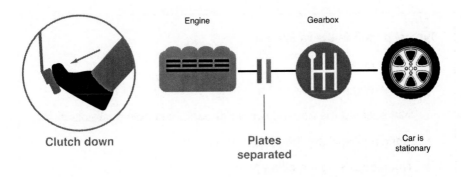

Clutch down   Engine   Gearbox

Plates
separated

Car is
stationary

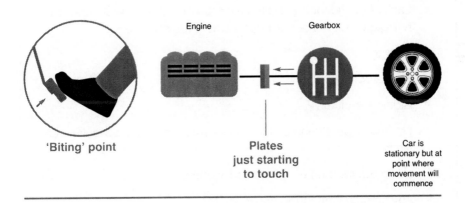

'Biting' point   Engine   Gearbox

Plates
just starting
to touch

Car is
stationary but at
point where
movement will
commence

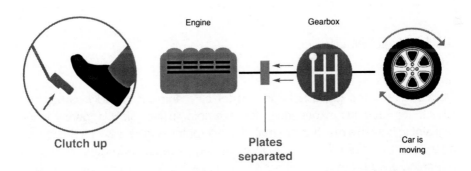

Clutch up   Engine   Gearbox

Plates
separated

Car is
moving

Typical clutch faults to expect

- Unsuitable footwear

- Forgetting to use the clutch where necessary

- Not pushing the pedal down far enough to enable gear selection

- Bringing the clutch pedal up too quickly

- Not recognising the biting point

- Setting the accelerator (gas) too low or too high

- Lack of confidence with clutch control resulting in precedence not being given to other road users where appropriate

- Stalling

- Kangarooing

- Riding the clutch

- Not using gas during clutch control for manoeuvring/moving very slowly

- Using the footbrake and clutch together

- Any combination of the above faults.

SKILLS DEVELOPMENT

Use of the gears

Correct use of the gears is important for safe and eco-friendly car control. Check for previous experience, for example, using bicycle gears when explaining how this mechanism makes work for the engine easier – the lowest gear (first) to move off and drive at a walking pace; second gear to drive at a running pace up to top gear for cruising speeds. You will normally need to demonstrate the palming technique (from the instructor's seat). Depending on how quickly your learner can pick up the skill, you may need to give various prompts, often repeatedly, until the skill is mastered.

how2become

Professional tip: Avoid physical contact with your learner's hand.

Instruction method: Practise makes perfect. To assist practise, below are some examples of questions that you might ask your learner. With experience you can devise your own bank of possible questions. Questions used must be appropriate to the learner and the circumstances of the lesson. Judge the balance of 'telling' and 'Q&A' on how the learner responds to your guidance.

EXAMPLE GEAR QUESTIONS

Introduction	Do you know what the manual gears do?
Manual gearbox	Do you know how many gears this car has and what each one does?
Neutral	What is neutral?
First gear	What gear will you normally pull away in?
Second and third gears	Which are your 'working' gears and when do you use them?
Fourth and fifth gears	When will you be able to use the higher gears and what benefits do they give you?
Power/Control & flexibility	Which gears have the greatest and least power?
Changing gear	How will you know when to change gear?
Block changes	Do you need to always change through each gear?
Technique	What technique will you use to select a gear?

Typical gear faults to expect

- Typical faults to anticipate – Not recognising neutral/first gear position

- Not selecting the gear intended

- Too tight or slack grip on the lever

- Incorrect technique for correct gear selection

- Hurried gear selection

- Slow gear changing up causing loss of speed

- Not recognising the need to change up or down gear as appropriate

- Changing up or down too early or too late

- Slipping the clutch in second (or higher gear)

- Unnecessary declutching or declutching too early

- Needlessly moving the steering to the left/right when changing gear

- Forgetting what gear has been selected and looking down at the gear lever.

SKILLS DEVELOPMENT

Use of the steering

Correct use of the steering is important to ensure that the car follows a safe and accurate course. To ensure this, learners need to look at the road well ahead and must not be allowed to develop the habit of looking down at the gears. The 'pull-push' way of steering can be practised between lessons using something with a circular shape, like a plate, that learners can run through their hands. Depending on how quickly your learner can pick up the skill, you may need to repeat your instruction frequently.

Professional tip: While correcting steering faults, avoid physical contact with your learner's hands.

Instruction method: Practise makes perfect. To assist practise, below are some examples of questions that you might ask your learner. With experience you can devise your own bank of possible questions. Questions used must be appropriate to the learner and the circumstances of the lesson. Judge the balance of 'telling' and 'Q&A' on how the learner responds to your guidance.

EXAMPLE STEERING QUESTIONS

Introduction	Have you seen this illustration before? (Use 'Driving – the Essential Skills')
Grip and hand position	How should you hold the steering wheel?
Driving a straight course	Where should you be looking?
Turning a corner	How should you turn the steering wheel?
"Pull-push" system	What are the advantages of 'feeding' the steering wheel through the hands?
Dealing with obstructions and bends	How much will you need to steer to clear?
Tyre pressures and load	What may make your steering wheel harder to turn?

Typical steering faults to expect

- Tight or slack grip

- High or low hands

- Steering when the car is stationary

- Allowing the steering wheel to spin back on its own

- Crossing the hands when forward turning

- Uneven and uncoordinated steering

- Under- or over-steering

- Inaccurate steering

- Short and shuffly steering (no 'lead' hand to begin turn).

THE REMAINING CONTROLS

Continue with the controls to be used when starting the engine – ignition key and switch (steering lock), ignition and oil warning light. You need only teach the essential controls. This means any ancillary control needed on the day by the learner e.g. wipers if it's raining, lights if it's dark.

ANCILLARY (MINOR) CONTROLS

Lights, horn, wipers, washers, air conditioning and/or fan (ventilation system), fuel and temperature gauges, warning lights, speedometer, rev counter, hazard lights, heated rear screen, rear fog lamps. This can also include the use of satellite navigation and any hands-free mobile phone system that is installed.

VISUAL CONTROLS

The importance of good clear visibility through the windows and the mirrors. Be aware of the blind areas caused by the pillars between the windscreen and the side doors. There will be times when you need to move your head to check the movement of other road users.

DUAL CONTROLS

Explain what these are and that you will inform the learner if and when you use them.

PROCEDURE FOR STARTING THE ENGINE

You're ready for your learner to drive for the first time. Move on to the next lesson plan 'Moving Away & Making Normal Stops'.

LESSON II: MOVING AWAY AND MAKING NORMAL STOPS

KEY LEARNING POINTS

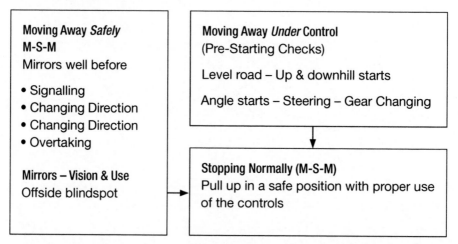

Moving Away *Safely*
M-S-M
Mirrors well before

- Signalling
- Changing Direction
- Changing Direction
- Overtaking

Mirrors – Vision & Use
Offside blindspot

Moving Away *Under* Control
(Pre-Starting Checks)

Level road – Up & downhill starts

Angle starts – Steering – Gear Changing

Stopping Normally (M-S-M)
Pull up in a safe position with proper use of the controls

Moving the car off for the very first time has to be one of the most exciting and memorable moments for the new learner driver. Talking your learner through the safe routine for moving off and stopping will usually require comprehensive guidance, known as 'full instruction'. This instruction must be clear and concise, with sufficient detail to enable your learner to carry out the exercise successfully. The words you use are important, as is the timing of the instruction.

STAGE OF ABILITY

- Untrained

RECAP

- 'Cockpit drill' (DSSSM)
- Controls Lesson

CORE OF THE LESSON

Decide in which order to brief and practise the skills to be learnt.

- Prepare. Getting the car ready to move off
- Observe. Making sure it is safe to move off
- Move. Coordinating the controls properly
- The 'Safety Line'. This is the correct road position. Decide the safest distance to be from the kerb or what clearance must be given to obstructions in the road such as parked vehicles.

PRACTISE

- A quiet road is ideal
- The ideal road for this exercise is an oval-shaped crescent with few parked vehicles.
- Learners must not be led into situations that they are not ready for.
- Learners will need to be talked through turning corners and any traffic situations that occur.
- Minimise inconvenience to other road users.

USE OF THE DUAL CONTROLS

Most learners will try their best to follow directions and instructions. Expect unintentional mistakes to happen.

It may well be necessary to use the dual controls or take hold of the steering wheel. Learners need to be told that this has been done and why the action was necessary.

PHRASEOLOGY

Instruction needs to be clear and unambiguous ie

- KEEP IT SHORT & SIMPLE!

Use clear phraseology. To ensure that it works, compare it with your own sequence of driving actions.

Moving away safely

The importance of observation:

- Ahead
- in the interior rear view mirror
- in the exterior mirrors and offside blindspot

First introduction to the 'Highway Code' Driving Plan

- Mirrors Signal Manoeuvre (MSM Routine)

Moving away under control

The importance of:

- not rolling back on an uphill start
- coordinating use of the clutch (biting point) with the accelerator (gas) correctly

Introduce the first steering exercise:

- an angle start

Moving along

The importance of using the mirrors well before:

- signalling
- changing speed
- direction
- overtaking

Stopping normally

The importance of pulling up:

- in a safe road position
- close to the kerb
- using the MSM routine

USEFUL LESSON HINTS

- Use an illustration

- When moving off, the most important places to look are all the mirrors, the offside blindspot and the direction of travel. A nearside blindspot check is unnecessary.

- Locate the place you want your learner to pull up during the briefing

- Dry runs. Consider running through the first attempt with the engine switched off

- Continue practising the exercise, including how and when to change gears.

PHRASEOLOGY – MOVING AWAY AND MAKING NORMAL STOPS

The following phraseology is an example of what you might need to say. Don't assume that this is all you have to say or exactly what you will need to say every time. Your learner may not do what you ask, so you may have to repeat a particular phrase in a different way. You may need to change the words to fit the:

a) way you speak

b) particular learner you are instructing

c) road and traffic conditions that prevail when you are using them

STARTING – ON A LEVEL ROAD

- **Prepare**   Handbrake applied

    Gear lever in neutral

    Start engine (release key as soon as it starts)

    Clutch down (keep it down)

    Left hand on gear lever – palm facing me

    Select first gear

    Set gas

- **Observe**   Check mirrors

    Check blindspot

    Check road ahead

    Check mirrors again

    Indicate right (if necessary)

- **Manoeuvre**   Release handbrake (when safe)

    Slowly clutch up

    When the car moves – keep your feet still

STEERING

- **Safety Line**   Steer (slightly) right, then

    Steer (slightly) left to the safety line

    Slowly clutch up fully

    Left foot on the floor

    Check mirrors

    A little more gas (if safe)

STOPPING

Just before/past the lamp post on the left, I would like you to park (Example)

Check Mirrors

Indicate left (if necessary)

Cover brake

Cover clutch

Steer (slightly) left towards the kerb

Steer right to a safe parking position

Gently brake

Clutch down

Gently brake to a stop – keep your feet still

Apply handbrake

Select neutral – rest feet

Cancel signal (if necessary)

Switch the engine off

AN ALTERNATIVE EXAMPLE OF INSTRUCTION FOR MOVING AWAY AND MAKING NORMAL STOPS:

Pre-starting checks and turn on the ignition. Press the clutch down and select first gear. Press down slightly on the accelerator and hold your foot steady, there should be enough power to hear the engine rev but not roar. Find the biting point by gradually easing up off the clutch until the car dips slightly and the engine noise drops. Keep your left foot still.

Before you move off, look in your rear view and door mirrors, and check over your right shoulder to make sure there's no danger in your blind spot. Think very carefully about whether you need to signal or not. Release the handbrake and let the clutch up slowly allowing you to move off.

Before you prepare to pull over, make sure it is safe to do so. Check the rear view, and then door mirrors. Give a signal if there's traffic close behind you or to let road users ahead know of your intentions, and slow your speed by easing your foot off the accelerator.

When pulling over, steer close and parallel to the kerb. Then brake gently until you have completely stopped, pressing down on the clutch as you do so. Secure the car by applying the handbrake, select neutral, and if you did signal now's the time ensure the indicators off.

The distance from the kerb is crucial – if you're too far, you could be an obstruction to passing road users; if your tyres scrape or touch the kerb, you're putting the safety of the vehicle's wheels at risk. Avoid positioning your car where you might inconvenience somebody else, such as in front of a driveway or near any kind of crossing or junction. This is just right.

UPHILL STARTS – AN EXAMPLE OF INSTRUCTION

Moving away from the kerb facing up a hill is trickier than on flat ground, as your car will naturally roll backwards – you have to control the car to prevent this happening.

Pre-starting checks and turn on the ignition. Press the clutch down and select first gear. Press down slightly on the accelerator and hold your foot steady, there should be enough power to hear the engine rev but not roar. Find the 'biting-point', by gradually easing up off the clutch until the car dips slightly and the engine noise drops. Keep your left foot still. Apply slightly more pressure than usual on the accelerator to overcome the slope of the road. If

you stall, don't panic; apply the handbrake, put the gear back to neutral, take a deep breath to calm your nerves, and start again.

Check your rear-view and door mirrors for other road users, with particular attention to any pedestrians that may be crossing behind your car. Check the blind spot over your right shoulder and, if necessary, signal. If it is safe to move off, release the handbrake and slowly ease off the clutch; enough to allow the car to start moving forward. Apply the accelerator, building up more momentum than usual in first gear to counteract the effects of the hill, and drive off into the road.

DOWNHILL STARTS – AN EXAMPLE OF INSTRUCTION

Moving away on a downhill slope is easier, as you can use gravity to aid your progress. However, you must take care to keep control of your vehicle, particularly on steep hills.

Pre-starting checks and turn on the ignition. Press down the clutch and put the car into the appropriate gear, first or second depending on the gradient of the slope. With the clutch down, fully apply the footbrake and release the handbrake.

Check it is safe to move off in the mirrors and don"t forget the blind spot. Indicate if necessary. When you"ve established it is safe to move off, slowly release the footbrake, and your car should begin to roll forward down the hill. Gently release the clutch and transfer your right foot from the brake to the accelerator, pulling into the road.

ANGLE STARTS – ON A LEVEL ROAD

If another car is parked close to your car, you may have to move off at a sharp angle. This procedure is similar to pulling away in a straight line, but you may need to move very slowly in order to give yourself time to steer. Keep the gas at an even rate and, as you let the clutch pedal up to the biting point, the car will start to move. A slight pressure on the clutch pedal will slow you down or bring the car to a stop again.

Ease the clutch up a fraction and you will creep forwards again. Then creep forwards or backwards a few inches at a time whenever you are in a confined space or need to edge forwards to see clearly.

Use the Mirrors-Signal-Manoeuvre (MSM) routine – look in your mirrors, especially the interior and right-door mirrors. If the road behind looks reasonably clear, have a look over your right shoulder into the area not covered by your mirrors – the blind spot. You are looking for vehicles, cyclists or pedestrians coming out of driveways or trying to cross the road. You also need to check the road ahead, making sure that oncoming vehicles aren't on your half of the road. Keep looking all around. Decide whether you need to signal. Before you move, have a final check all around, including blind spots, to make sure that it is still safe.

PHRASEOLOGY – GEAR CHANGES

Depending on your estimate of your learner's ability, you may decide to go through a dry run before live practise.

Example – Gear change up, first to second

- We are now going to select second gear
- Check mirrors, if safe, a little more gas
- Cover clutch
- Hand on gear lever palm towards me
- Clutch down, off gas
- Select second gear
- Slowly clutch up with a little gas
- Check mirrors, if safe, a little more gas

Adapt this phraseology for changing from second to third gear; third to fourth and fourth to fifth gear.

Example – Gear change down third to second

- We are now going to select second gear
- Check mirrors, if safe, gently brake, off brake
- Cover clutch
- Hand on gear lever palm towards me
- Clutch down, off gas (if necessary)

- Select second gear

- Slowly clutch up with a little gas

For initial practice, learners should be introduced to changing down through each gear, but for normal driving they need to be taught block changes, eg fourth to second and third to first as appropriate.

MOVING AWAY AND MAKING NORMAL STOPS – SKILLS DEVELOPMENT

Success depends on developing the skill of controlling the clutch to ensure a safe and smooth drive.

Recap on the previous explanation that the clutch is the link between the engine and the gears. Eg "When you press the clutch pedal you disconnect this link and therefore the engine runs freely without any drive ... when you move off, you need to learn to bring the clutch into play so that the engine can drive the car. This takes practise and the more you have, the better you will become at moving off and gear changing, smoothly".

Instruction Method: Below are some examples of questions that you might ask your learner when they have practised this exercise sufficiently. With experience you can devise your own bank of possible questions. Questions used must be appropriate to the learner and the circumstances of the lesson. Judge the balance of 'telling' and 'Q&A' on how the learner responds to your guidance.

Topic Key Point:	Sample Question:
Pre-starting checks	Before starting the engine what safety checks must you make?
Moving Off Under Control	How will you co-ordinate the controls to move away?
Preparation	Is the road flat or are we on a slope?
Coordination	Will you need clutch or footbrake control to move off?
Moving Off Safely	Where will you need to look before moving off?

Use of Mirrors	What do you look for in the mirrors?
Right-shoulder check	How can you check the blind spot to your immediate right?
Use of Signals	When will you need to indicate?
Road Positioning	How will you judge your distance from the pavement as you're moving along?
Normal Stop	Where and how are you going to pull in and park?
Mirrors	Before stopping what is the first thing that you must you do?
Signal	When will we need to signal before pulling up?
Manoeuvre	How will you use the controls when pulling up?
Position	Where will you stop and how far from the kerb should you be?

Typical faults to anticipate

Not making effective use of the mirrors before:	Moving off; signalling; changing direction; overtaking; slowing or stopping
	Not looking over the right shoulder before moving off.
	Not signalling or signalling incorrectly
	Stalling
	Rolling back when moving off uphill and/or 'kangarooing'
	Pulling up in an unsafe position
Gear changing	Mis-selection of gears and poor coordination with gas and clutch
	Loss of road speed when changing up

LESSON III: USE OF MIRRORS

KEY LEARNING POINTS

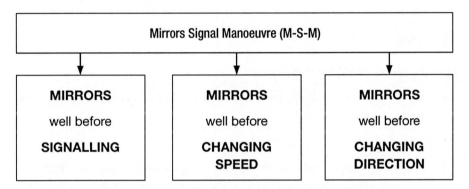

"To know where you're going, you have to know where you've been."

A good driving style depends on a full awareness of not only what can be seen ahead, but also, what is happening on both sides and behind the car.

STAGE OF ABILITY

- Partly-Trained

RECAP

- Use of Mirrors

CORE OF THE LESSON

- How will you link previous learning?

- Does your learner know why:

  - the mirrors must be checked on particular occasions?
  - it is necessary and important to look over the right shoulder before moving off?

- Does your learner know:

  - which mirror(s) to use and when?
  - what to look for in the mirror(s)?
  - the different types of glass used in the interior and exterior mirrors?

PRACTISE

- Use of the MSM Driving Plan

Development of hazard recognition. Just looking in the mirrors is not enough. Learners must see what is there

- Mirrors – The importance of:

  - checking for traffic following closely by using the interior mirror
  - use of the outside mirrors when and where necessary.

- Using the appropriate mirrors well before:

  - signalling
  - changing speed
  - changing direction
  - overtaking.

PHRASEOLOGY

Probably the most frequently used instruction phrase is:

"Mirrors – off gas."

Typical instruction may be:

"Check mirrors before you…"

Develop this instruction to:

"What's following behind?"

"What is the vehicle behind doing now?"

"What can we do about the closely following driver?"

USEFUL LESSON HINTS:

- Use the illustrations in 'Driving – The Essential Skills' to introduce or review the key lesson points.

- Making unnecessary head movements to check the interior mirror is wrong and potentially dangerous.

- On an ADI Part 3 test you will also be expected to deal with the emergency stop in the same period.

  Plan your time efficiently. Be guided by any local knowledge.

  Begin with a short recap on use of mirrors.

  On the drive to the emergency stop site, give corrective instruction on use of mirrors where this is needed.

USE OF MIRRORS – SKILLS DEVELOPMENT

To be able to respond safely to hazards ahead, drivers need to know what traffic is doing behind and to the sides of the car. The system of driving taught to new drivers is taken from the 'Highway Code'. "Mirrors Signal Manoeuvre" (MSM) provides the foundation of every driving instructor's lesson plan. This routine provides the driving plan for all hazards and is the foundation of the System of Car Control advocated by expert advanced drivers.

Instruction Method: Below are some examples of questions that you might ask your learner. With experience you can devise your own bank of possible questions. Questions used must be appropriate

to the learner and the circumstances of the lesson. Judge the balance of 'telling' and 'Q&A' on how the learner responds to your guidance

Topic Key Point:	Sample Question:
Mirrors	Where must you regularly check as you drive along?

Set up – vision	How did you set the mirrors as part of your cockpit drill?
Types of glass	What are the two types of glass used and how does this affect what you can see in each mirror?
Blindspot	What does the offside mirror help minimise?
Driving plan	What is the first aspect of your driving plan?
Mirror use	When, specifically, must you use your mirrors?
Effective use	Why is just checking the mirrors not enough?

Typical faults to anticipate

Not setting or adjusting the mirrors from a normal driving seat position.

Ineffective use of mirrors before:

- signalling
- changing direction
- changing speed
- overtaking.

LESSON IV: USE OF SIGNALS

KEY LEARNING POINTS

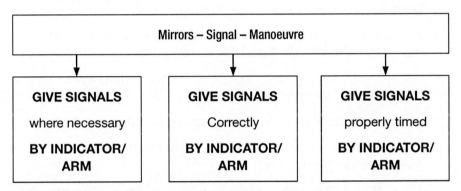

Signals are the most obvious means of communication between drivers and all other road users. They are usually given by direction indicator but can also be given by arm. Sometimes we complain about the lack of signals from other drivers. We should, instead, identify how a driver's intention may be determined by where he or she is looking, the vehicle's speed and position, or the direction where the front wheels are pointing.

STAGE OF ABILITY

- Partly-Trained

RECAP

- Use of signals

What knowledge does your learner have about using the indicator for

signalling? What are the other ways that the vehicle can indicate a driver's intention to head in a particular direction?

CORE OF THE LESSON

- How will you link previous learning?

USEFUL LESSON HINTS:

- Use the illustrations in the 'Highway Code' and 'Driving – The Essential Skills' to introduce or review the key lesson points.
- Encourage the thoughtful use of signals, including the use of arm signals to reinforce normal use of indicators.
- Anticipate the meaning of brake lights or hazard warning lights as a signal from vehicles in front.
- Include correct use of the horn when moving or stationary.
- The acceptability of courtesy signals (such as raising the left hand to thank another driver).
- On an ADI Part 3 test you will also be expected to deal with pedestrian crossings in the same period.

ADDITIONAL USEFUL LESSON HINTS:

- Teach the meaning of signals given by other road users by:
  - Flashing the headlamps.
  - Arm (particularly pedal cyclists and horse riders).

PHRASEOLOGY

"Indicate left."

"Indicate right."

Develop this instruction to:

"Do you need to signal before moving away?"

"At what point will you need to signal?"

"Has your signal cancelled?"

SKILLS DEVELOPMENT

Correct signals must be given where they are needed and in plenty of time. This skill is a key element of the system of driving taught to new drivers and developed by expert advanced drivers – Mirrors Signal Manoeuvre (MSM). MSM provides the foundation of every driving instructor's lesson plan.

Instruction Method: Below are some examples of questions that you might ask your learner when they have practised sufficiently. With experience you can devise your own bank of possible questions. Questions used must be appropriate to the learner and the circumstances of the lesson. Judge the balance of 'telling' and 'Q&A' on how the learner responds to your guidance.

Topic Key Point:	Sample Question:
Signals by direction indicator	How do you normally communicate with other road users?
Signal use	When will you usually need to indicate?
Signal timing	At what point should any necessary signal be given?
Correct signals	What must you ensure about your signal?
Signals by arm	When might you need to give an arm signal?
Arm signal use	How do arm signals help other road users?
Use by other road users	Which road users can only use arm signals?

Typical faults to anticipate

- Signals not given correctly, in good time or where necessary
- Unnecessary signals.

Finally, as with all driving practise under instruction, complete the instructional core competencies by being sure that your learner knows and understands the causes of any driving faults and the solutions that you have provided.

LESSON V: EMERGENCY STOP

KEY LEARNING POINTS

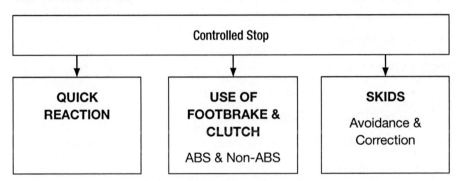

Having instructed an untrained learner to move off and make a normal stop, you need to decide on which lesson to introduce the emergency stop exercise.

With good anticipation there should seldom be a need for any driver to have to perform an emergency stop as opposed to a normal stop. Other road users do make mistakes that can create emergency situations, for instance, a child running out into the road. Where a learner is also taking private practise, and as this will probably be in a car without dual controls, you should introduce this exercise sooner rather than later in the course of lessons. This lesson and subsequent practise must take place well before the day of the driving test.

STAGE OF ABILITY

- Partly-Trained

RECAP

- Anticipation and Normal Stops

CORE OF THE LESSON

- Quick reaction

The importance of reacting promptly to your "Stop" signal.

- Use of footbrake

The importance of braking firmly and recognising the ABS pulsating.

- Use of clutch

The acceptability of simultaneously depressing the clutch in an ABS vehicle maintaining car control and stability.

- Skid avoidance

The importance of:

  - assessing the condition of the road surface
  - using the car's controls properly.

- Skid correction
- The importance of:

  - identifying the different types of skid
  - removing the cause of the skid
  - using the car's controls to correct the skid

PRACTISE

- Chose a very quiet road and ensure that there is no following traffic
- Link previous knowledge about anticipation and normal stops to this lesson. This should include theory knowledge eg:

  - a car's shortest stopping distances
  - that stopping distances increase greatly at higher speeds or on slippery road surfaces

PHRASEOLOGY

Your phraseology is quite simply:

"Stop!"

You should then instruct your learner to:

"Carry on driving" (when safe).

Try to correct any fault(s) on the move, otherwise direct your learner to:

"Pull up in a convenient place."

USEFUL LESSON HINTS:

- On a driving test this exercise is marked/assessed in the 'controlled stop' category

- Ensure that you choose a suitable site for the exercise. The standard signal we use is to raise the right hand level above the knee, facing forwards, and say "STOP" loudly. Before you give this signal, make sure that you have checked your instructor's dual mirror and over your own right shoulder.

- Dry runs. Consider running through the first attempt while the vehicle is stationery with the engine switched off. Check for your learner accidentally pressing the gas pedal.

- Providing that the learner shows ability, it is acceptable to practice this exercise at speeds over 30mph, providing that the location is safe and the speed is within the legal limit.

- Use the illustrations in the 'Driving – The Essential Skills' to help you to introduce skid correction. Skid control is a specialist area of driving. Keep to the basics, you do not need to go into great detail at this stage of learning to drive.

- Once the exercise is complete, do not debrief while still blocking the road.

- Do move to a safe position on the left before assessing the performance.

- Ensure that your learner looks over both shoulders before moving away.

- On an ADI Part 3 test you will also be expected to instruct on the general use of the mirrors in the same lesson period. When formatting your lesson plan you should therefore ask about any previous instruction on the use of mirrors.

THE EMERGENCY STOP – SKILLS DEVELOPMENT

Reading the road well ahead will develop good hazard perception skills. No driver is perfect and there can be a need sometimes to have to perform an emergency stop. Learners must be encouraged to adapt a post-test driving style that does not rely on repeated heavy braking.

All new cars have had anti-lock brakes (ABS) fitted following a European Union mandate that came into force in July 2004. New drivers may well buy a car manufactured before this time, so you do need to cover the braking technique in a car not fitted with ABS.

Instruction Method: Below are some examples of questions that you might ask your learner. With experience you can devise your own bank of possible questions. Questions used must be appropriateto the learner and the circumstances of the lesson. Judge the balance of 'telling' and 'Q&A' on how the learner responds to your guidance.

Topic Key Point:	Sample Question:
Importance	When might you have to carry out an emergency stop?
Stopping distances	Do you know your shortest stopping distances?
Reaction time	How will you need to respond to the emergency?
Braking	How will you need to brake?
De-clutching	When should you de-clutch?
Handbrake	When should you apply the handbrake?
Hands	Where must your hands be when you stop?
Skid causation	What are the main causes of skids?

how2become

Skid avoidance	How can we avoid a skid?
Types of skid	What types of skid are there?
Skid correction	How would you correct each type?

Typical faults to anticipate

- Panicking
- Not reacting promptly
- Braking too hard or too gently
- Simultaneously braking and de-clutching (non-ABS car)
- Applying the handbrake before the vehicle has stopped
- Not keeping both hands on the steering wheel when stopping
- Not recognising the condition of the road surface and/or correcting any skid
- Using the mirrors before stopping
- Not moving away safely after the exercise.

LESSON VI: APPROACHING JUNCTIONS – MAJOR TO MINOR

KEY LEARNING POINTS

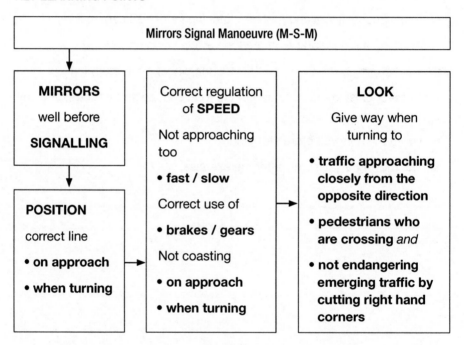

Keeping to the Driving Plan, Mirrors – Signal – Manoeuvre (MSM) is a simple and easy way to ensure success when teaching learners to drive. MSM is the common theme throughout most of the driving lessons that you will deliver. It is first introduced during the moving off and stopping exercise, then it will be repeated during the next lesson, approaching junctions.

Where possible, the location chosen should lend itself to turning from major roads to minor roads before commencing on emerging at junctions.

STAGE OF ABILITY

- Partly-Trained

RECAP

- Any previous attempts at turning corners
- Steering technique – following a safety line keeping a safe distance from the kerb and any parked cars or obstructions. Agree on use of pull-push/ rotational steering techniques.

CORE OF THE LESSON

- Decide whether you are going to teach left or right turns first, or will you teach both together?
- Does you learner know how to locate a turn?
  - Breaks in the building or hedge line
  - Street furniture
  - Road markings
- Anticipation
  Being prepared to give way before turning to pedestrians who are crossing the road

---

Mirrors Signal Manoeuvre (MSM)

The need to use the 'MSM Driving Plan' – a safe system of approach

Mirrors

The importance of

- checking for traffic following closely by using the interior mirror
- using the outside mirrors when and where necessary

Signal

The importance of signalling:

- in good time
- for the benefit of traffic/pedestrians that can or cannot yet be seen

---

Position

The importance of:

- being in the correct road position for turning left or right
- making sure for yourself that it is safe for your learner to steer into any new position for turning
- watching for your learner swinging out before turning left or staying over to the left before turning right from a wide road

Speed

The importance of:

- instructing your learner to use the correct amount of gentle braking to bring the speed down in enough time to select and engage the gear – probably second (though not always)
- watching your learner to ensure that the clutch isn"t pushed down before or when turning the corner (not coasting).

Look

The importance of observation. Look:

- ahead for traffic approaching closely
- into the minor road for pedestrians who are crossing
- in the appropriate exterior mirror for any overtaking vehicles
- for your learner steering too soon causing the kerb to be mounted or a corner to be cut

USEFUL LESSON HINTS

- Use illustrations as frequently as you feel necessary.
- Try and teach left turns first if you can (You are less likely to need to stop!)
- Decide how the point of turn and the amount of steering differs between sharp and gentle corners.
- Teach the Pull-Push steering technique recommended in the 'Driving – The Essential Skills'

- If your learner continues to struggle with steering around a corner offer a demonstration

PHRASEOLOGY

The following concise phraseology is an example of what you might need to say. Don't assume that this is all you have to say or exactly what you will need to say every time. Your learner may not do what you ask, so you may have to repeat a particular phrase in a different way. You may need to change the words to fit the:

1. way you speak

2. particular learner you are instructing and

3. road and traffic conditions that prevail when you are using them.

TURNING LEFT – MAJOR TO MINOR

		Take the next road on the left
•	Mirrors	Check the interior mirror first
•	Signal	Indicate left
•	Position	Maintain safety line
•	Speed	Less gas / gently brake
		Off brake
		Select second gear
•	Look	(Check left door mirror)
		Check ahead and look left
		At the corner, steer left
		Two-thirds of the way round
		Steer right to keep to the safety line
		Check mirrors
		If safe, a little more gas

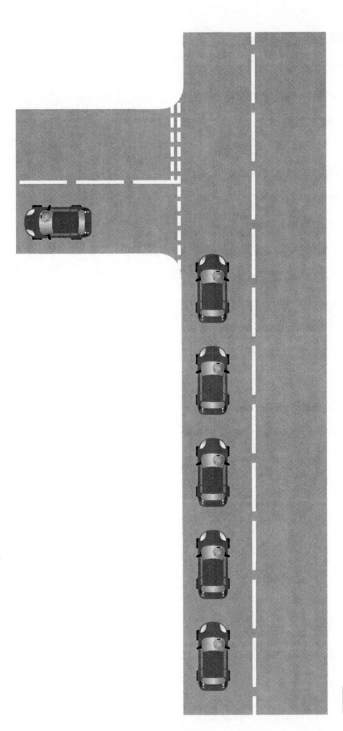

TURNING RIGHT – MAJOR TO MINOR

	Take the next road on the right
• Mirrors	Check the interior mirror first
• Signal	Indicate right
• Position	Position just left of centre
• Speed	Less gas / gently brake
	Off brake
	Select second gear
• Look	(Check right door mirror)
	Check ahead and look right
	Towards the centre of the side road, steer right
	Two-thirds of the way round
	Steer left to keep to the safety line
	Check mirrors
	If safe, a little more gas
	Select third gear (if appropriate)

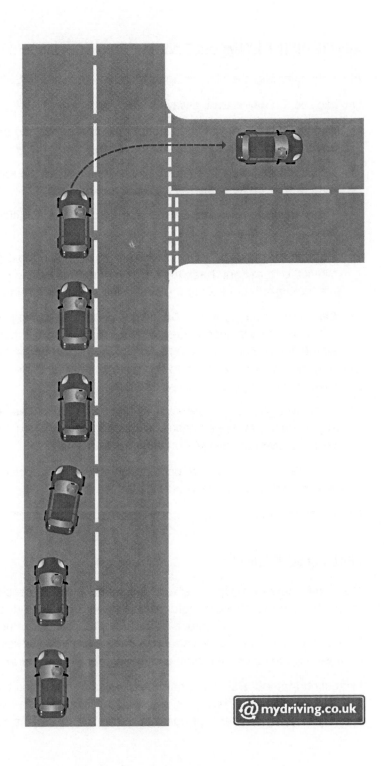

AN ALTERNATIVE EXAMPLE OF INSTRUCTIONAL GUIDANCE/COMMENTARY

All junctions require the Mirrors Signal Manoeuvre routine (MSM) on approach.

You can see the turn ahead, always check your:

- Mirrors first; begin with your interior rear-view mirror and then check your door mirror on the side you are turning.

- Signal; do this even if you can"t see anyone else on the road. There may well be traffic in the road you are turning into.

- The manoeuvre is broken down into three sections: Position, Speed and Look.

- Position the car depending on whether you are going to go straight on, turn left or turn right. Keep the car in your normal driving position if you are turning left, or close to the centre line if you are turning right.

- Slow your speed by easing off the gas pedal and braking sufficiently. It is usual to be in second gear when turning off from a main road, although if you are turning right and have to cross oncoming traffic, you may need to change down to first gear. If necessary, use the footbrake to stop completely until it is safe to turn.

- Look. What do you see? As well as oncoming traffic, keep checking for any obstacles and pedestrians. Is it safe to go or do you need to give way to other road users? Complete the turn safely.

Once you have joined the new road, straighten the car's position and ensure that your indicator signal is turned off.

Check your mirrors and continue at an appropriate speed.

SKILLS DEVELOPMENT

Most traffic collisions happen at road junctions. This is because they are the most common place where motor vehicles and other road users come into close proximity with each other. To reduce this risk, judgements must be based on best practice and instructors have a professional responsibility to exercise full control of the lesson and the learner's likely actions.

Instruction Method: Below are some examples of questions that you might ask your learner when they have practised sufficiently. With experience you can devise your own bank of possible questions. Questions used must be

appropriate to the learner and the circumstances of the lesson. Judge the balance of 'telling' and 'Q&A' on how the learner responds to your guidance.

Topic Key Point:	Sample Question:
Types	What types of junction do you know of?
Location	How do you spot a junction?
Mirrors	How do you check for following traffic?
Signal	When should you state your intention?
Position	At what point should you position correctly?
Speed	When will you slow by deceleration/ braking?
Gear	At what point will you change gear?
Look	Before turning where must you check and what are you looking for?

Typical faults to anticipate

- Not recognising the junction in time
- Not making effective use of the mirrors well before signalling or changing direction
- Checking mirrors and signalling/changing direction simultaneously
- Incorrect position on approach
- Positioning too late
- Approaching too fast/slow
- Not braking sufficiently before gear changing
- Coasting
- Not giving way to pedestrians who are crossing or approaching traffic when turning right

And finally, as with all driving practise under instruction, complete the instructional core competencies by being sure that your learner knows and understands the causes of any driving faults and the solutions that you have provided.

LESSON VII: APPROACHING JUNCTIONS – MINOR TO MAJOR

KEY LEARNING POINTS

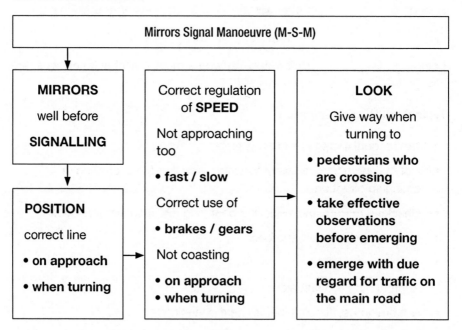

Mirrors Signal Manoeuvre (M-S-M)		
MIRRORS well before **SIGNALLING** **POSITION** correct line • **on approach** • **when turning**	Correct regulation of **SPEED** Not approaching too • **fast / slow** Correct use of • **brakes / gears** Not coasting • **on approach** • **when turning**	**LOOK** Give way when turning to • **pedestrians who are crossing** • **take effective observations before emerging** • **emerge with due regard for traffic on the main road**

Teach the Driving Plan, Mirrors – Signal – Manoeuvre (MSM). MSM is the common theme throughout most of the driving lessons that you will deliver. Beginning with the moving off and stopping exercise, then it is repeated when instructing on approaching junctions, whether you are teaching your learners to turn into or emerge out of.

STAGE OF ABILITY

- Partly-Trained

RECAP

- Any previous attempts at emerging minor to major

Depending on your locality, your learner should normally have turned left and right several times from major to minor roads. You will then be in a position to transfer previous learning to this new subject.

CORE OF THE LESSON

- Decide whether you are going to teach left or right turns first, or will you teach both together?
- Give way before emerging to pedestrians who are crossing the road
- Waiting behind the double broken white lines in order to give way to any approaching traffic
- Judgement of the speed and distance of any approaching traffic

---

Mirrors Signal Manoeuvre (MSM)

The need to use the 'MSM Driving Plan' – a safe system of approach

Mirrors

The importance of

- checking for traffic following closely by using the interior mirror
- use of the outside mirrors when necessary

Signal

The importance of signalling:

- in good time
- for the benefit of traffic/pedestrians that can or cannot yet be seen

---

Position

The importance of:

- being in the correct road position for turning left or right
- making sure for yourself that it is safe for your learner to steer into any new position for turning
- watching for your learner swinging out before turning left or staying over to the left when turning right from a wide road

Speed

The importance of:

- instructing your learner to use the correct amount of gentle braking to bring the speed down in time to select and engage the right gear. This will probably be first (though not always).
- watching your learner to make sure that the clutch pedal is not pressed down too early on the approach (not coasting)

Look

The importance of zones of vision. Watch for:

- road markings. Are they 'Give Way' or 'Stop'
- overtaking vehicles in the appropriate exterior mirrors
- pedestrians who are crossing the road
- motorcyclists – Do 'Think Bike!'
- your learner NOT making the necessary observations in both directions

Ensure that your learner does not cause another vehicle to change speed or direction when emerging

USEFUL LESSON HINTS:

- Where possible, teach major to minor turns before introducing this exercise
- Start by teaching left turns first if you can (because these are easier).
- Use the Prepare – Observe – Manoeuvre (POM) Routine (introduced

during the move away exercise) as the procedure for emerging at junctions.

- Decide how the "point of turn" and amount of steering may vary at different junctions.

- Continue to use the (Pull-Push) steering technique recommended in the 'Driving – The Essential Skills'.

PHRASEOLOGY

The following concise phraseology is an example of what you might need to say. Don't assume that this is all you have to say or exactly what you will need to say every time. Your learner may not do what you ask, so you may have to repeat a particular phrase in a different way. You may need to change the words to fit the:

1. way you speak

2. particular learner you are instructing and

3. prevailing road and traffic conditions.

LEFT – MINOR TO MAJOR

	Take the next road on the left
Mirrors	Check the interior mirror first
Signal	Indicate to the left
Position	Maintain safety line
Speed	Less gas / gently brake
	As there is limited vision, be prepared to stop at the broken white lines
	(Check left door mirror)
	Steer slightly to the left
	Select first gear
Prepare	Have the car ready to move off
Look	Take effective observations (looking both ways)
Observe	Move forwards under clutch / brake control
Move	Steer left and then right to the safety line
Check mirrors	If safe, a little more gas
	Select second gear

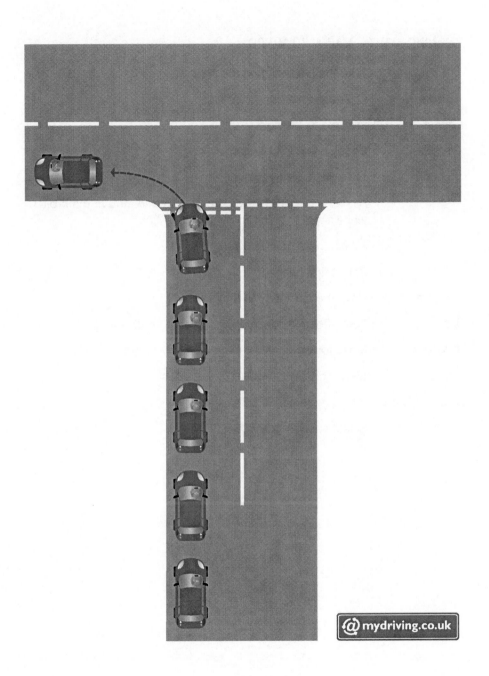

TURNING RIGHT – MAJOR TO MINOR

	Take the next road on the right
Mirrors	Check the interior mirror first
Signal	Indicate to the right
Position	Position just left of centre
Speed	Less gas / gently brake
	As there is limited vision, be prepared to stop at the broken white lines
	(Check right door mirror)
	Select first gear
Prepare	Have the car ready to move off
Look	Take effective observations (Looking both ways)
Observe	Move forwards under clutch / brake control
Move	Steer right and then left to the safety line
Check mirrors	A little more gas (if safe)
	Select second gear

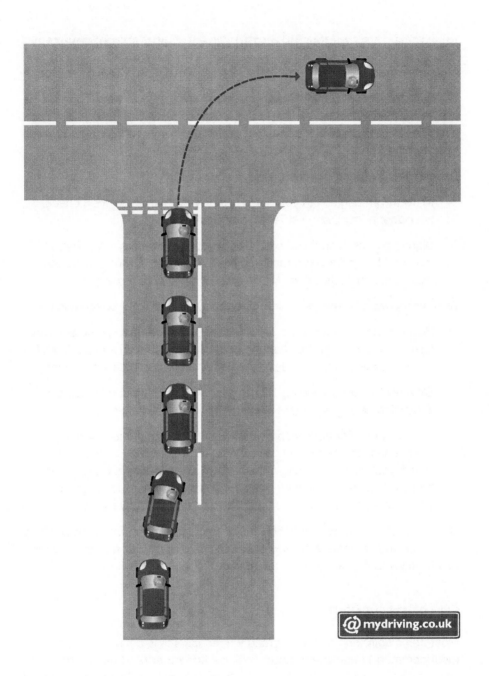

AN ALTERNATIVE EXAMPLE OF INSTRUCTIONAL GUIDANCE/COMMENTARY

All junctions require the Mirrors Signal Manoeuvre routine (MSM) on approach.

When turning onto a main road you must always give way. This will be shown by the broken white line at the junction. However, if there is a solid white line you must always come to a complete stop, whether there is traffic approaching or not.

You can see the junction ahead, always check your:

- Mirrors first; begin with your interior rear-view mirror and then check your door mirror on the side you are turning.

- Signal; do this even if you can't see anyone else on the road. There may well be traffic in the road you are turning into. Giving a direction indicator signal lets others know which way you are turning.

The manoeuvre is broken down into three sections: Position, Speed and Look:

- Position the car depending on whether you are going to go straight on, turn left or turn right. Position the car in your normal driving position if you are turning left, or close to the centre line if you are turning right.

- Slow your speed by easing off the gas pedal and braking sufficiently. It is usual to select first gear when emerging onto a main road.

- Look carefully for approaching traffic as you reach the junction. If you need to wait for more than a short time for a big enough break in the traffic, you will need to apply the handbrake. It is always better to be patient, and wait for a bigger gap in the traffic, rather than causing a dangerous situation or causing other road users inconvenience.

Once you have emerged onto the major road, straighten the car's position. Do ensure your indicators are switched off, make an interior mirror check and gently accelerate to an appropriate speed.

SKILLS DEVELOPMENT

Most traffic collisions happen at road junctions. This is because they are the most common place where motor vehicles and other road users come into close proximity with each other. To reduce this risk, judgements must be based on best practice and instructors have a professional responsibility to exercise full control of the lesson and the learner's likely actions.

Instruction Method: Below are some examples of questions that you might ask your learner when they have practised sufficiently. With experience you can devise your own bank of possible questions. Questions used must be appropriate to the learner and the circumstances of the lesson. Judge the balance of 'telling' and 'Q&A' on how the learner responds to your guidance.

Topic Key Point:	Sample Question:
Types and Location	What are the types of junction and how do you spot them?
Mirrors	How do you check for following traffic?
Signal	When should you state your intention?
Position	At what point should you position correctly?
Speed	When will you slow by deceleration/ braking?
Gear	At what point will you change gear?
Look (Approach)	What is your 'Zone of Vision'?
Look (Observation)	What type of road user must you look out for?
Look (Emerging)	What must you avoid when emerging?

Typical faults to anticipate

- Not recognising the junction in time

- Not making effective use of the mirrors well before signalling or changing direction

- Checking mirrors and signalling/changing direction simultaneously

- Incorrect position on approach

- Positioning too late

- Approaching too fast/slow

- Not braking sufficiently before gear changing. Coasting

- Not looking both ways on approach

- Not giving way to pedestrians who are crossing

- Not properly observing 'Give Way' or 'Stop' lines

- Emerging without due regard for approaching traffic / undue hesitancy

And finally, as with all driving practise under instruction, complete the instructional core competencies by being sure that your learner knows and understands the causes of any driving faults and the solutions that you have provided.

LESSON VIII: CROSSROADS

KEY LEARNING POINTS

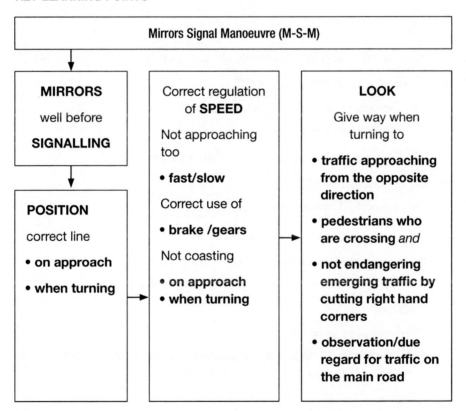

Mirrors Signal Manoeuvre (M-S-M)

MIRRORS

well before

SIGNALLING

POSITION

correct line

• **on approach**

• **when turning**

Correct regulation of **SPEED**

Not approaching too

• **fast/slow**

Correct use of

• **brake /gears**

Not coasting

• **on approach**
• **when turning**

LOOK

Give way when turning to

• **traffic approaching from the opposite direction**

• **pedestrians who are crossing** *and*

• **not endangering emerging traffic by cutting right hand corners**

• **observation/due regard for traffic on the main road**

The Driving Plan, Mirrors – Signal – Manoeuvre (MSM) is the common theme throughout most of the driving lessons that you will deliver. It should be taught when instructing on all approaches to road junctions including crossroads.

how2become

STAGE OF ABILITY

- Partly-Trained

RECAP

- Dealing with Junctions

Before going onto Crossroads your learner should normally have turned left and right several times from major to minor roads and minor to major roads. You will then be in a position to transfer previous learning to the new subject.

CORE OF THE LESSON

- How will you link previous knowledge about junctions to crossroads?
- What are you going to teach first?
  - Proceeding ahead with/without priority
  - Turning left or right with/without priority
- Will you have to start by teaching a mix of these?
- How will you deal with:
  - Unmarked Crossroads / Traffic Lights

Mirrors Signal Manoeuvre (MSM)

The need to use the 'MSM Driving Plan' – a safe system of approach

Mirrors

The importance of:
- checking for traffic following closely by using the interior mirror
- use of the outside mirrors when necessary

Signal

The importance of signalling:
- in good time
- for the benefit of traffic/pedestrians that can or cannot yet be seen

---

Position

The importance of:

- being in the correct road position for
    - proceeding ahead or turning left
    - turning right taking into account
        - the type and size of the crossroads
        - the movement of any approaching traffic
- making sure for yourself that it is safe for your learner to steer into any new position for turning

Do watch your learner for positioning faults!

Speed

The importance of:

- instructing your learner to use the correct amount of gentle braking to bring the speed down in time to select and engage the gear
- watching for your learner coasting

Look

The importance of zones of vision. Watch for:

- pedestrians who are crossing
- traffic from any direction including
    - emergency vehicles
    - stolen vehicles
- overtaking vehicles viewed in either of the exterior mirrors
- your learner NOT making the necessary observations

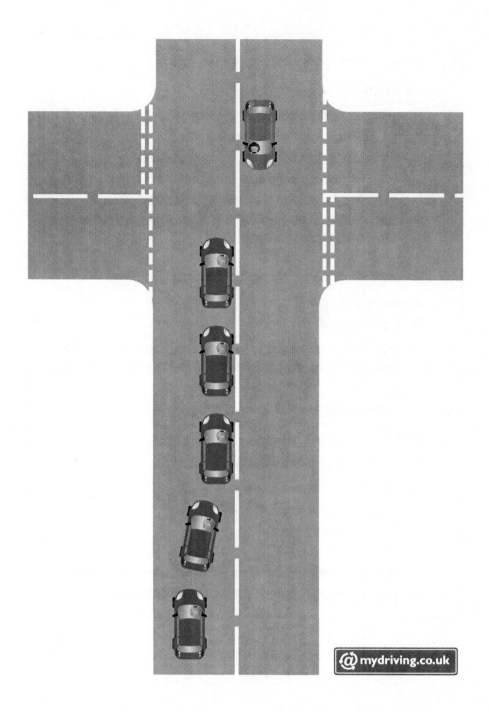

how2become

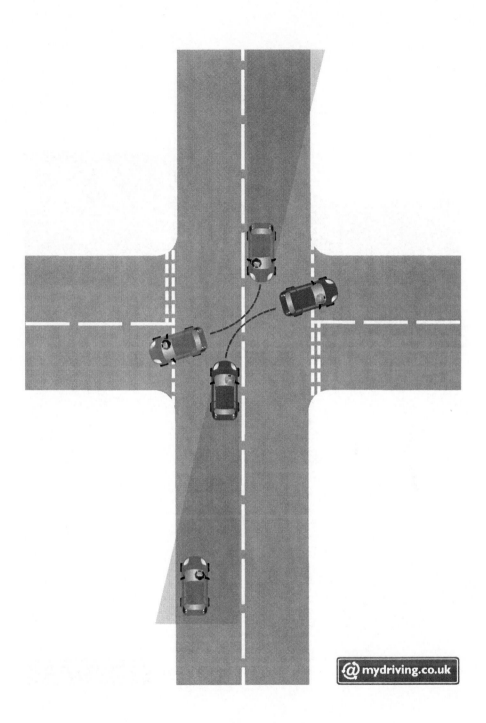

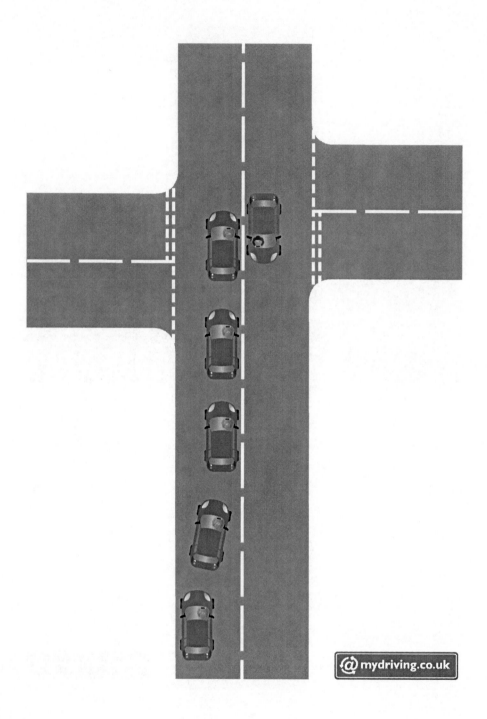

how2become

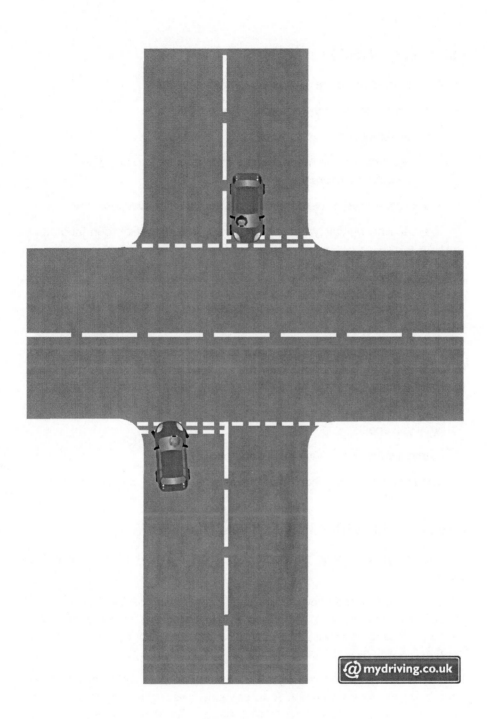

USEFUL LESSON HINTS:

- Use illustrations as frequently as you feel necessary
- Focus the lesson on the correct:
  - observations
  - responses to be made (eg to turn right offside to offside or nearside to nearside)
- Having practised crossroads your learner can then progress onto:
  - dealing with all types of roundabout, including mini-roundabouts

PHRASEOLOGY

Adapt junction phraseology to suit different road and traffic situations at crossroads.

Don"t assume that this is all you have to say or exactly what you will need to say every time. Your learner may not do what you ask, so you may have to repeat a particular phrase in a different way. You may need to change the words to fit the:

1. way you speak
2. particular learner you are instructing and
3. road and traffic conditions that prevail when you are using them.

AN EXAMPLE OF INSTRUCTIONAL GUIDANCE/COMMENTARY

Crossroad layouts vary so pay careful attention to road markings and traffic signs.

As you approach, remember: mirrors, signal, and get in position. Reduce your speed even if you are travelling ahead, and keep looking. Observation is the key to safety at crossroads, be prepared for the unexpected – vehicles don"t always give way or stop as we would.

Take extra care when turning right if an approaching vehicle is also turning right. You can either turn nearside to nearside, passing passenger doors, or offside to offside, passing driver's side doors. The choice depends on the

size and the shape of the junctions, the road markings and the position of the vehicles. Get eye-contact with the approaching driver, this helps to determine who might go first.

SKILLS DEVELOPMENT

Crossroads are a type of road junction. There are different kinds of crossroads, some may or may not have road markings and others may be controlled by traffic lights. You must be sure that your learners have reached a stage of ability where they are ready and able to follow your instructions, especially if the crossroads is complex.

Instruction Method: Below are some examples of questions that you might ask your learner when they have practised sufficiently. With experience you can devise your own bank of possible questions. Questions used must be appropriate to the learner and the circumstances of the lesson. Judge the balance of 'telling' and 'Q&A' on how the learner responds to your guidance.

Topic Key Point:	Sample Question:
Types	What types of crossroads have you come across?
Location	How do you spot crossroads?
Mirrors	How do you check for following traffic?
Signal	When should you state your intention before a turn?
Position	At what point should you position correctly?
Speed	When will you slow by deceleration/braking?
Gear	At what point will you change gear?
Look (Approach)	Where must you always look on your approach?
Look (Position – Turning Right)	Where will you need to position when turning right?
Look (Observation)	What type of road user must you look out for?
Look (Emerging)	What must you avoid when emerging?

Typical faults to anticipate

- Not recognising the crossroads in time.
- Not making effective use of the mirrors well before signalling or changing direction.
- Checking mirrors and signalling/changing direction simultaneously.
- Incorrect position on approach.
- Positioning too late.
- Approaching too fast/slow.
- Not braking sufficiently before gear changing. Coasting.
- Inappropriate position for turning right.
- Not giving way to pedestrians who are crossing.
- Not properly observing 'Give Way' or 'Stop' lines.
- Emerging without due regard for approaching traffic/undue hesitancy.

The DSA do not have a Pre-Set ADI Test that specifically covers roundabouts. Many roundabouts are converted crossroads, designed specifically to help keep traffic moving. Where possible, move on to teach all types of roundabouts, once you have covered and practiced crossroads sufficiently.

Finally, as with all driving practise under instruction, complete the instructional core competencies by being sure that your learner knows and understands the causes of any driving faults and the solutions that you have provided.

LESSON IX: APPROACHING ROUNDABOUTS

KEY LEARNING POINTS

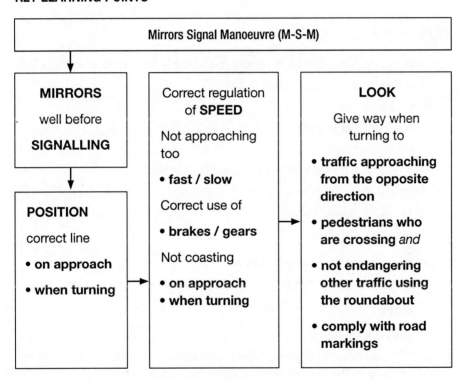

Many roundabouts are converted crossroads, designed specifically to help keep traffic moving. The Driving Plan, Mirrors – Signal – Manoeuvre (MSM) should be taught when instructing on all approaches to road junctions including roundabouts.

STAGE OF ABILITY

- Partly-Trained

RECAP

- Dealing with junctions including crossroads

Before going onto roundabouts your learner should normally have been introduced to and practised T-junctions and crossroads. You will then be in a position to transfer previous learning to the new subject.

CORE OF THE LESSON

- How will you link previous knowledge about junctions to roundabouts?
- What are you going to teach first?
  - Turning left
  - Proceeding ahead
  - Turning right
- Will you have to start by teaching a mix of these?
- How will you deal with:
  - Mini-roundabouts

Mirrors Signal Manoeuvre (MSM)

The need to use the 'MSM Driving Plan' – a safe system of approach

Mirrors

The importance of:

- checking for traffic following closely by using the interior mirror
- use of the outside mirrors when necessary

Signal

The importance of signalling:

- in good time
- for the benefit of traffic/pedestrians that can or cannot yet be seen

---

Position

The importance of:

- being in the correct road position for
  - turning left
  - proceeding ahead
  - turning right
    - the type and size of the roundabout
- the movement of approaching traffic, particularly from the right

Speed

The importance of:

- instructing your learner to use the correct amount of gentle braking to bring the speed down in time to select and engage the gear
- watching for your learner coasting

Look

The importance of zones of vision. Watch for:

- pedestrians who may be crossing the approach to the roundabout or exit roads
- traffic crossing in front of you – most importantly vehicles that are going to leave at the next exit
- traffic straddling lanes or positioned incorrectly
- motorcyclists
- cyclists and horse riders (who must stay in the left hand lane but signal right if they intend to go around the roundabout
- long vehicles – they may have to move across several lanes, so be careful and watch for their signals.

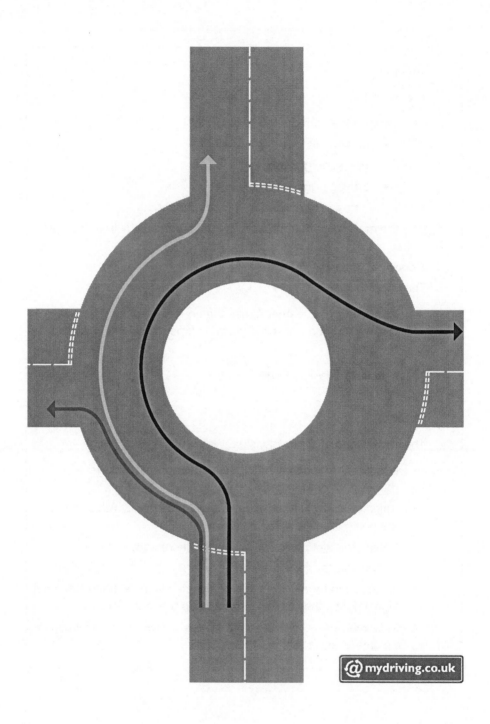

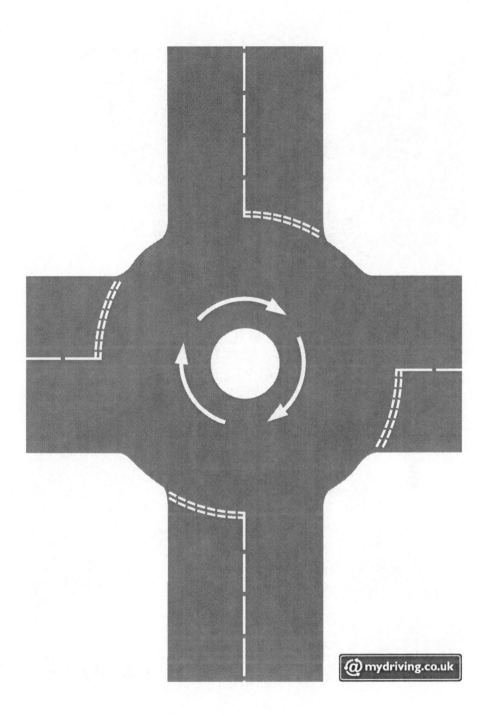

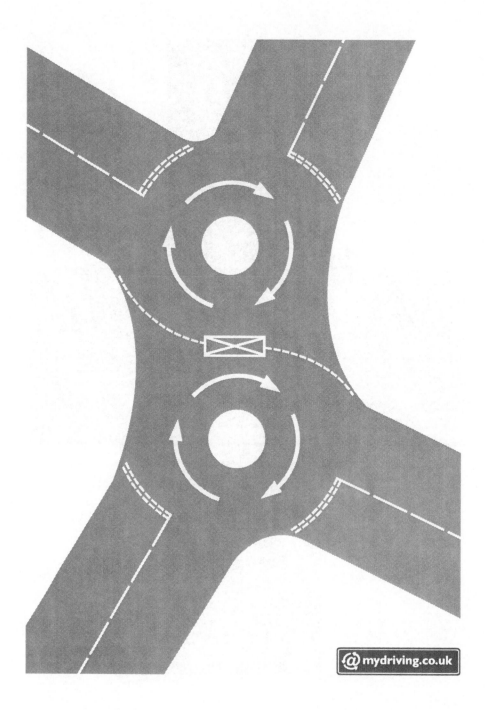

USEFUL LESSON HINTS

- Use illustrations as frequently as you feel necessary. Refer directly to the 'Highway Code' for advice on turning left, going straight on and turning right

- Focus the lesson on the correct:

  - Observations. On approach to many roundabouts there should be a direction sign that will indicate the shape of the roundabout and how many exits there are in total. Checking the mirrors is important, but also watch the car in front of you. Many crashes at roundabouts occur as drivers rear-end the car in front of them. This is because they are watching the traffic on the roundabout not the traffic waiting to get on it. Make sure the vehicle has actually moved away before your learner starts to move forward.

  - Speed and gear. On approach, get these correct and if the way is clear, on many occasions your learner will be able to merge with the moving traffic without stopping.

  - Response. Always keep an eye on your mirrors but most importantly watch the car in front of you. Also what other cars are telling you with their indicators might not be what they are actually about to do!

- Explain that mini-roundabouts follow the same 'Highway Code' rules as bigger roundabouts. Also, when it comes to multiple and satellite roundabouts systems, deal with each separately, treating it as you would treat a normal roundabout.

PHRASEOLOGY

Adapt junction phraseology to suit different road and traffic situations at roundabouts.

Don't assume that this is all you have to say or exactly what you will need to say every time. Your learner may not do what you ask, so you may have to repeat a particular phrase in a different way. You may need to change the words to fit the:

1. way you speak

2. particular learner you are instructing and

3. road and traffic conditions that prevail when you are using them.

AN EXAMPLE OF INSTRUCTIONAL GUIDANCE/COMMENTARY ...

Introduction:

"As with all junctions roundabouts require the Mirrors Signal Manoeuvre routine on approach. The manoeuvre is broken down into 3 sections; Position, Speed and Look.

- Position the car depending on what exit you are intending to take.

- Slow your speed by easing off the gas pedal, braking sufficiently and then select the appropriate gear to match your speed.

- Look. What do you see? Is it safe to go or do you need to give way to other traffic?"

Turning Left:

"When approaching roundabouts positioning is crucial, it helps to tells people what your intentions are. If you are taking the first exit, keep to the left side of the road, and indicate left. Slow down and be prepared to give way, and as always, keep looking to anticipate the actions of other road users. Stay in the left lane when using the roundabout ready to easily leave at the first exit"

Going straight ahead:

"If you are going straight ahead, again keep left and stay in the left lane. Be aware of other traffic at all times, don"t forget some will be turning off before you, or will need to move to the left lane too. Once you"ve just passed the exit before the one you"re leaving at indicate left. Make good use of you nearside door mirror ensuring you there is no one who will be inconvenienced by you turning off."

Turning Right:

"If you're turning right, stay over to the right on your approach and indicate as such. Keep to the right lane and maintain the signal on the roundabout. Once you have passed the exit before the one you want change your signal, and making good use of your nearside mirror, move over to the left hand lane. Once you have left the roundabout, make sure your signal has been cancelled and check for following traffic in your mirrors."

SKILLS DEVELOPMENT

Roundabouts are a type of road junction. They are in effect, one-way systems that allow motorists to move more freely with the flow of traffic and tend not to create large backlogs of traffic, as traffic lights can do.

There are different kinds and sizes of roundabout. Also, at the point of entry, some may have a single broken white line, while in busier locations, roundabouts are more likely to have a double broken white lines road markings. The meaning of these should be explained.

You must be sure that your learners have reached a stage of ability where they are ready and able to follow your instructions, especially if the crossroads is complex.

Instruction Method: Below are some examples of questions that you might ask your learner when they have practised sufficiently. With experience you can devise your own bank of possible questions. Questions used must be appropriate to the learner and the circumstances of the lesson. Judge the balance of 'telling' and 'Q&A' on how the learner responds to your guidance.

Topic Key Point:	Sample Question:
Types	What types of roundabouts have you come across?
Location	How do you spot roundabouts?
Mirrors	How do you check for following traffic?
Signal	When should you state your intention before a turn?
Position	At what point should you position correctly?
Speed	When will you slow by deceleration/braking?
Gear	At what point will you change gear?
Look (Approach)	Where must you always look on your approach?
Look (Position – Turning Right)	Where will you need to position when turning right?
Look (Observation)	What type of road user must you look out for?
Look (Emerging)	What must you avoid when emerging?

Typical faults to anticipate

- Not recognising the roundabout in time.

- Not making effective use of the mirrors well before signalling or changing direction.

- Checking mirrors and signalling/changing direction simultaneously.

- Incorrect position on approach.

- Positioning too late.

- Approaching too fast/slow.

- Not braking sufficiently before gear changing. Coasting.

- Inappropriate position for turning right.

- Not giving way to pedestrians who are crossing.

- Not properly observing "Give Way" lines.

- Emerging without due regard for traffic already established on the roundabout.

- Not anticipating traffic from the right waiting for traffic from ahead.

- Undue hesitancy.

Finally, as with all driving practise under instruction, complete the instructional core competencies by being sure that your learner knows and understands the causes of any driving faults and the solutions that you have provided.

LESSON X: PEDESTRIAN CROSSINGS

KEY LEARNING POINTS

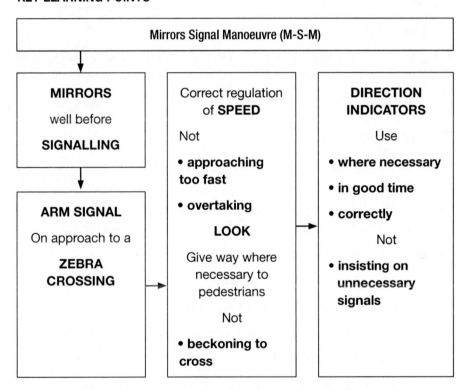

Outside the car we are all pedestrians. Last year, traffic collisions involving pedestrians accounted for 453 deaths, 5,454 reported serious injury casualties and 20,291 slightly injured casualties. This represents a 1% increase on 2010, where the overall pedestrian casualty figure was 25,845.

Road safety is very much the business of driving instructors. Stressing the role of planning ahead while driving and reducing speed to match the risks is

part of our everyday tasks. Pedestrians don't need licences! The number of collisions that take place before or after the actual crossing would suggest that a lack of preparation, both on the approach and prior to moving off again is a significant contributory factor.

STAGE OF ABILITY

- Partly-Trained

RECAP

- Dealing with pedestrian crossings

How much knowledge, as a pedestrian, does your learner have about pedestrian crossings? How much of this knowledge can be transferred to the new subject?

CORE OF THE LESSON

- How will you link previous knowledge about pedestrian crossings to the lesson?

- How many types of pedestrian crossing are there to teach? Zebra, Pelican, Puffin, Toucan, Equestrian and School Crossing Patrol.

- Does your learner know:

    - what each type has in common?

    - how to identify each type of crossing?

    - the sequence of the lights at controlled pedestrian crossings?

    - the status of refuges?

    - about not overtaking or parking within the zig-zag lines?

    - about leaving the crossings clear in traffic queues?

Mirrors Signal Manoeuvre (MSM)

The importance of having a safe system of approach.

Mirrors

The importance of

- checking for traffic following closely by using the interior mirror
- use of the outside mirrors when necessary

Arm Signal

The importance of:

- giving a slowing down arm signal on approach to a zebra crossing where people are waiting to cross, in good time, where it is necessary

Position

Normal road postioning

Speed

The importance of instructing your learner to use the correct amount of gentle braking to bring the speed down in time to give way, not overtaking on approach to, or within, the zig-zag lines.

Look

The importance of:

- continuous observation. Both you and your learner must watch carefully the conduct of pedestrians near the crossing and those using the crossing.

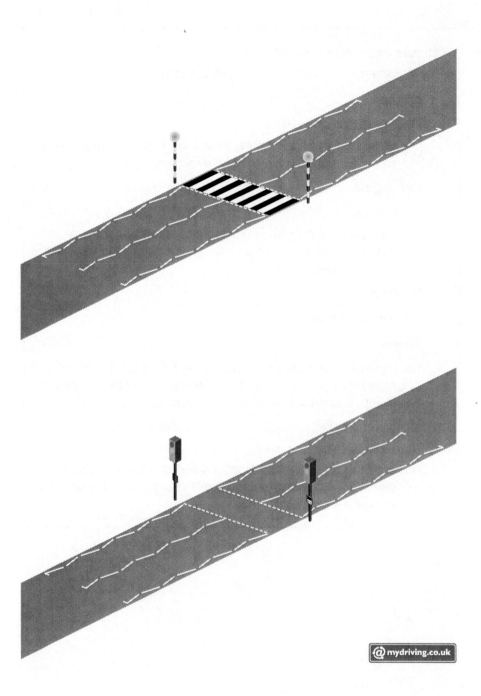

how2become

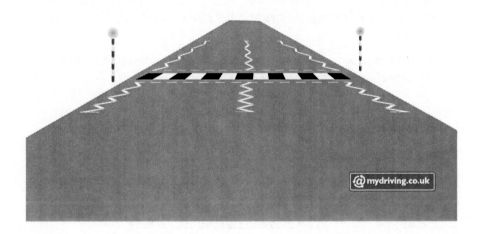

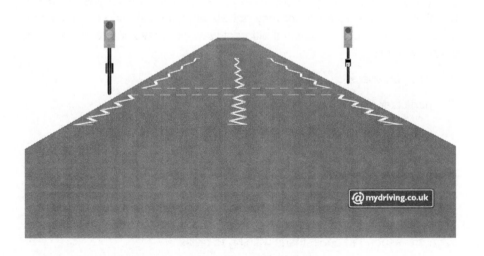

USEFUL LESSON HINTS

- Use illustrations as frequently as you feel necessary. When dealing with not overtaking you can also check that your learner knows why it is illegal to park within the zig-zag lines.

- On an ADI Part 3 test you will also be expected to deal with the use of direction indicator signals and all other arm signals briefly, in the same period.

- Do refer directly to the 'Highway Code' for information on the penalties for pedestrian crossing related offences.

PHRASEOLOGY

"In town, window down!"

Adapt your phraseology to suit the different road and traffic conditions at pedestrian crossings. For example:

"What type of pedestrian crossing can you see ahead?"

"Is there any traffic following behind you?"

"Will you need to give way at the pedestrian crossing?"

"When will you be able to begin moving off again?"

Don't assume that this is all you have to say or exactly what you will need to say every time. Your learner may not do what you ask, so you may have to repeat a particular phrase in a different way. You may need to change the words to fit the:

1. way you speak

2. particular learner you are instructing

3. road and traffic conditions that prevail when you are using them

SKILLS DEVELOPMENT

This exercise is intended to ensure that learners have an adequate knowledge of the different types of pedestrian crossing, along with an ability to judge and correctly respond to pedestrians wishing to cross.

Instruction Method: Below are some examples of questions that you might ask your learner when they have practised sufficiently. With experience you can devise your own bank of possible questions. Questions used must be appropriate to the learner and the circumstances of the lesson. Judge the balance of 'telling' and 'Q&A' on how the learner responds to your guidance.

Topic Key Point:	Sample Question:
Types of pedestrian crossing	Give me some examples of different types of pedestrian crossing. (Zebra, Pelican, Puffin, Toucan, Equestrian and school crossings)
Beacons, lights and zig-zag lines	How do you spot a pedestrian crossing?
Pedestrian safety	Where must you look on the approach?
Children and the elderly	Who is most at risk crossing the road?
Mirrors	Where do you check first?
Signal	What signal could you give?
Manoeuvre	At what speed should you approach?
Not overtaking or parking	What must you not do within the zig-zag lines?
Giving way	When must you give way?
Leaving crossing clear	What should you not do on the crossing?
Pelican crossing	What does the flashing amber light mean?
Puffin crossing	What is the sequence of lights at a Puffin crossing?
Toucan crossing	What other type of road user will cross at a Toucan crossing?

Typical faults to anticipate

- Not showing recognition of the crossing or nearby pedestrians.
- Not applying the MSM routine.
- Speed too high on the approach.
- Not giving way where necessary.
- Stopping on crossing.
- Beckoning pedestrians to cross.
- Waiting needlessly at flashing amber lights.

Finally, as with all driving practise under instruction, complete the instructional core competencies by being sure that your learner knows and understands the causes of any driving faults and the solutions that you have provided.

LESSON XI: AWARENESS AND ANTICIPATION

KEY LEARNING POINTS

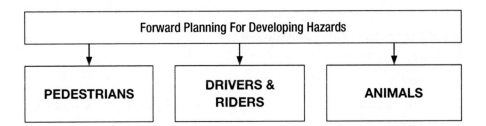

Being 'aware' and able to 'anticipate' is the main way for avoiding costly collisions.

Driving hazards can come singly or in clusters, they may overlap and change at any time, so, the training route must suit your learner's level of ability. Your learner needs to be able to cope, under instruction, with any new traffic situations that you introduce. To help your learner deal with any demanding situations you must always be ready to give them full instructional guidance.

STAGE OF ABILITY

- Partly-Trained

RECAP

- Use of the MSM routine when approaching developing hazards.

CORE OF THE LESSON – AWARENESS AND ANTICIPATION (FORWARD PLANNING)

When approaching

- Pedestrians

- Riders, such as pedal and motorcyclists

- Drivers of cars, vans, lorries and buses

- Horses and other animals

Does your learner know how to recognise situations and show restraint by holding back where necessary? How are you able to assist your learner's decision-making/problem solving?

Mirrors Signal Manoeuvre (MSM)

The Driving Plan

Mirrors

The importance of checking for traffic following closely in both interior and exterior mirrors.

Signal

The importance of using the direction indicators where necessary.

Manoeuvre

The importance of the correct line position, speed and continuous observation.

Look Assess Decide (LAD)

To apply the Driving Plan effectively we must ...

Look

... well ahead. Continuously observe the hazards, particularly those that might move and prioritise the most important.

Assess

... weigh up the whole traffic situation.

Do you need to prompt or talk the learner through the situation?

> **Decide**
>
> Decisions depend on a combination of
>
> 1. What can be seen
>
> 2. What cannot be seen
>
> 3. What you can reasonably expected other road users to do
>
> … what feedback do you have from your learner?
>
> … what do you expect your learner to do?
>
> … what intervention do you need to make, if any?

USEFUL LESSON HINTS:

- Use illustrations as frequently as you feel necessary.

- On an ADI Part 3 test 'awareness and anticipation' will be combined with at least two other lesson topics from the list – meeting; crossing; overtaking; adequate clearances and following distances, within the same lesson period.

PHRASEOLOGY

Adapt your phraseology to suit different road and traffic situations. For example:

"What do you expect the driver in front to do?"

"Do you think that pedestrian will step out into the road without looking first?"

"Is that cyclist likely to try and get past?"

SKILLS DEVELOPMENT

Combined with a positive attitude towards driving, the ability to show awareness and anticipation of all road and traffic situations is the key to achieving a collision free driving career.

While learning to drive, both learners and professional instructors have

how2become

their attention concentrated on observation and planning for all possible eventualities. The driving plan, 'Mirrors-Signal-Manoeuvre' (MSM) is essential to this skill development.

In practice, this needs to be linked with the learner's theory preparation, which is the Multiple-Choice Questions (MCQ) and 'Hazard Perception' video clips.

Instruction Method: Below are some examples of questions that you might ask your learner when they have practised sufficiently. With experience you can devise your own bank of possible questions. Questions used must be appropriate to the learner and the circumstances of the lesson. Judge the balance of 'telling' and 'Q&A' on how the learner responds to your guidance.

Topic Key Point:	Sample Question:
Anticipation	What is meant by anticipation?
What to look for	What are the developing hazards?
Pedestrians	What dangers are there from people walking?
Riders	What dangers are there from those people riding on two wheels?
Drivers	What dangers do other drivers of other vehicles present?
Animals	What other dangers can animals on the road present?
Weather and visibility	How can the weather affect your visibility or the road surface?
Driving Plan	What is the best routine for coping with a hazard?
Judgement	How will we make the correct responses to the traffic situations we come across?

Typical faults to anticipate

- Not applying the MSM routine.

- Driving too fast to be able to anticipate danger.

- Unnecessary emergency stops and/or continuous heavy braking.

- Failing to respond properly to the likely actions of other drivers, cyclists and pedestrians.

- Caught by surprise by a foreseeable danger.

- Not giving precedence to pedestrians or traffic where appropriate.

- Indecisiveness when dealing with other drivers who flash their headlamps.

- Not considering or using the horn/flashing headlamps where necessary.

- Increasing speed when being overtaken by another road user.

Finally, as with all driving practise under instruction, complete the instructional core competencies by being sure that your learner knows and understands the causes of any driving faults and the solutions that you have provided.

LESSON XII: JUDGEMENT WHEN: MEETING & CROSSING APPROACHING TRAFFIC; OVERTAKING, CLEARANCES & FOLLOWING DISTANCES

KEY LEARNING POINTS

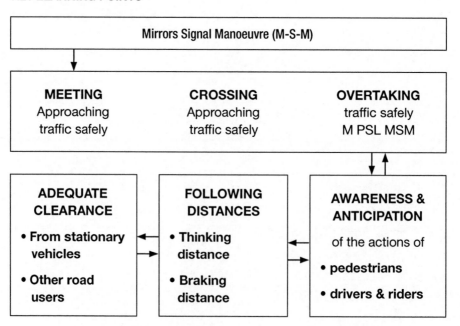

Meet and Cross Approaching Traffic

The ability to read the road ahead accurately and make correct judgements is particularly needed when meeting and crossing approaching traffic.

STAGE OF ABILITY

- Partly-Trained

RECAP

- Meeting traffic and crossing traffic

Your learner will have already dealt with cross traffic situations when turning right from major to minor roads. How did your learner get on? Is there any other previous learning that can be transferred from turning right at road junctions.

CORE OF THE LESSON

- Does your learner know the meaning of the terms 'meet' and 'cross traffic'?

- Judgement of the speed and distance of approaching traffic (awareness and anticipation of other traffic).

Mirrors Signal Manoeuvre (MSM)

Use of the MSM Driving Plan – The importance of having a system of approach.

Mirrors

The importance of checking for traffic following closely in both interior and exterior mirrors.

Signal

The importance of indicating correctly when turning right and not giving any misleading signals.

Position

The importance of a correct line of approach. If positioned correctly, there is usually no need to signal to pass parked vehicles. Re-check the mirrors in case vehicles behind misjudge the situation.

how2become

> **Speed**
>
> The importance of being able to stop in the distance seen to be clear.
>
> **Look**
>
> The importance of continuous observation. Looking out for situations where you need to give way.

USEFUL LESSON HINTS:

- Use illustrations as frequently as you feel necessary.

- Where a residential road is made narrow by parked cars on both sides, the correct road position can be to drive over the crown of the road.

- The 'Highway Code' offers very clear official advice on the meaning of headlamp flashing.

Always encourage your learner to remember that it is better to 'give' way than 'take'!

- On an ADI Part 3 test you will also be expected to deal with awareness and anticipation in the same lesson period.

PHRASEOLOGY

Adapt your phraseology to suit different road and traffic situations. For example:

"On which side of the road are the parked vehicles?"

"If another driver approaches what will you do?"

"Where is your holdback position?"

"If you proceed through the gap, are you likely to cause the approaching driver to slow down?"

"This is a crossing traffic situation ... will it be safe for you to turn or had you better wait?"

"If you turn now, will you cause the approaching driver to slow down?"

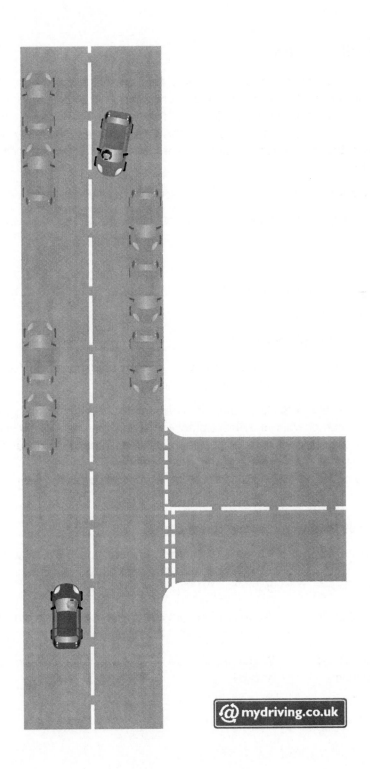

SKILLS DEVELOPMENT

With the increasing number of parked cars on residential roads, meeting approaching traffic is an important practical skill. Along with crossing approaching traffic, when turning right from a main road into a side road, learner drivers need to develop an ability to judge and correctly respond to these traffic situations. Practice needs to relate to the learner's theory preparation.

For effectiveness, this should also be linked with "awareness and anticipation".

Skill development demands a positive driving attitude. The necessary skills are:

- observation
- assessing what can be seen
- making decisions
- taking the right action

We also have to view the driver's attitude in terms of responsibility for actions and also their consideration for other road users.

Instruction Method: Below are some examples of questions that you might ask your learner when they have practised sufficiently. With experience you can devise your own bank of possible questions. Questions used must be appropriate to the learner and the circumstances of the lesson. Judge the balance of 'telling' and 'Q&A' on how the learner responds to your guidance.

Topic Key Point:	Sample Question:
Meeting traffic	If a vehicle is coming towards you in a road where parked cars make the road narrow, what should you do?
Crossing traffic	When turning right into a side road with a vehicle approaching, what must you avoid?
Awareness and anticipation	Which hazards are likely to affect you in the road ahead?

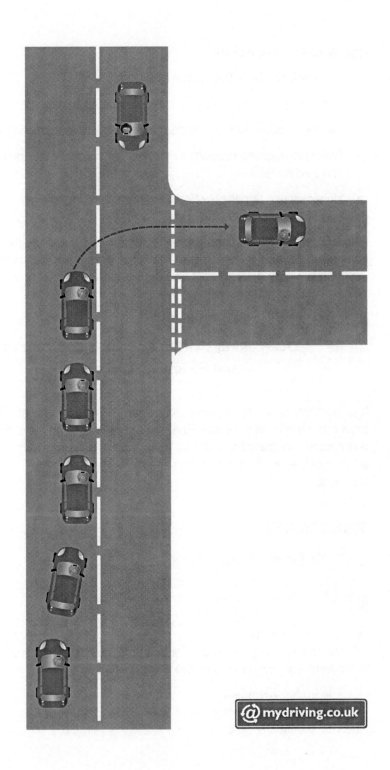

Typical faults to anticipate

- Not applying the MSM routine.

- Not giving precedence to oncoming traffic where appropriate.

- Turning right in front of approaching traffic where inappropriate.

- Failing to respond properly to the likely actions of other drivers, cyclists and pedestrians.

- Unnecessary signalling when passing parked vehicles.

Finally, as with all driving practise under instruction, complete the instructional core competencies by being sure that your learner knows and understands the causes of any driving faults and the solutions that you have provided.

Overtaking Traffic, Adequate Clearances and Following Distances

It is most important to overtake only where it is safe to do so. The ability to pass other traffic without danger and also leave enough room when clearing obstructions in the road, such as parked cars, calls for both very early and good anticipation of all the various situations that can present themselves on the road.

STAGE OF ABILITY

- Partly-Trained

RECAP

- Overtaking traffic
  Passing moving vehicles – For example, how has your learner overtaken any bicycles or milk floats before?

- Adequate clearances
  Passing stationary objects – For example, does your learner driver

leave enough room to accommodate a car door being accidentally opened or a pedestrian in a hurry, stepping out into the road?

In moving or stationary traffic, does your learner drive too close or too far from the vehicle in front?

CORE OF THE LESSON – OVERTAKING TRAFFIC

- Recognition of safe situations for overtaking

    Is it necessary to overtake?

    Is it safe ahead and behind?

- Link road speed with reaction times and braking distances
- Planning and ability to judge traffic situations

Position Speed Look – Mirrors Signal Manoeuvre (PSL-MSM)

The importance of having a system for overtaking.

Mirrors

Checking for traffic following closely in both interior and exterior mirrors.

Position

Not being so close to the vehicle in front that the view ahead becomes restricted, but close enough if the manoeuvre will be safe.

Speed

Changing down to the correct gear where necessary.

Look

Continuous observation of the road well ahead and for any approaching traffic.

Mirrors

Checking again for following traffic.

Signal

Using the direction indicators where necessary.

Manoeuvre

Correct line for overtaking; overtaking quickly and continuous observation.

CORE OF THE LESSON – ADEQUATE CLEARANCES AND FOLLOWING DISTANCES

- Keep plenty of space

    From parked cars and other obstructions, such as road works.

    Correct gap from vehicles in front – In moving traffic, being capable of stopping within the distance seen to be clear.

    In stationary traffic, where there is a car in front, being able to see the rear tyres and an amount of the road surface.

Clearances and following distances

The importance of:

Having an 'escape route'.

Where to steer to avoid the danger and having a collision.

Keeping the correct following distance.

Best practice is to use the separate distances given in the 'Highway Code'.

Be able to convert these distances between metric and imperial versions, as well as compare the gaps with distances such as those between street lamp posts or other lighting on other types of road.

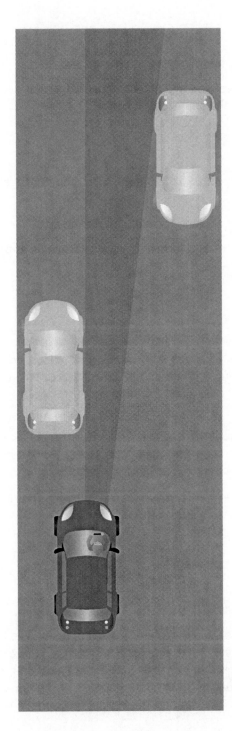

USEFUL LESSON HINTS:

- Use illustrations as frequently as you feel necessary
- On an ADI Part 3 test you will also be expected to deal with awareness and anticipation in the same lesson period

PHRASEOLOGY

Adapt your phraseology to suit different road and traffic situations. For example:

> "What is the danger of being too close to parked cars?"

> "Are you keeping tyres and tarmac in view between us and the car in front?"

SKILLS DEVELOPMENT

Overtaking stationary or moving vehicles can be hazardous, as can be a failure to keep proper clearances and following distances. Misjudgement in such situations may bring a driver into close conflict or actual collision with another driver or other road user. Practise needs to relate to the learner's theory preparation.

We also have to view the driver's attitude in terms of responsibility for actions and also their consideration for other road users. For effectiveness, this should also be linked with awareness and anticipation.

Skill development demands a positive driving attitude. The necessary skills are:

- observation
- assessing what can be seen
- making decisions
- taking the right action

Instruction Method: Below are some examples of questions that you might ask your learner when they have practised sufficiently. With experience you can devise your own bank of possible questions. Questions used must be appropriate to the learner and the circumstances of the lesson. Judge the balance of 'telling' and 'Q&A' on how the learner responds to your guidance.

Topic Key Point:	Sample Question:
Overtaking traffic	What is the correct routine for overtaking?
Clearances	What is the minimum distance for passing a parked vehicle in a residential road?
Following distances	What is the danger of getting too close to the vehicle in front?
Awareness and anticipation	What is the first action you should take when you see any hazard that might make you slow down or change direction?

Typical faults to anticipate:

- Not applying the PSL-MSM routine.
- Driving too close to other road users and/or parked vehicles.
- Following other vehicles too closely.

Finally, as with all driving practise under instruction, complete the instructional core competencies by being sure that your learner knows and understands the causes of any driving faults and the solutions that you have provided.

LESSON XIII: USE OF SPEED, MAKING PROGRESS AND ROAD POSITIONING

KEY LEARNING POINTS

SPEED	ROAD POSITIONING
Not driving too fast	Correct for the circumstances
• **legal limits** • **road conditions** • **traffic conditions**	**Not** • **too wide from the left** • **too close to the left**
MAKING PROGRESS	**Correct use of**
Not driving too slowly	• **lane discipline**
• **avoiding undue hesitancy by proceeding where safe** • **keeping up with the traffic flow within the legal limits**	

Speed is often blamed for vehicle collisions and the injuries or fatalities that occur as a result.

We live an on-demand world where we expect everything fast, whether it is the shortest flight times to foreign destinations or the food we eat. If we're asked to name the best driver in the world, our automatic choice is normally one of the fastest Formula 1 racing drivers.

As Approved Driving Instructors we are in a strong position to influence new drivers about their choice and use of speed once they have gained their full driving licence.

STAGE OF ABILITY

- Trained

RECAP

- Use of speed, making progress and road positioning

How will your lesson introduction differ for a learner at this stage?

Because each of these topics will have already been covered to a large extent during training, any briefing should normally be kept very short and concise.

Has your learner failed a driving test on these topics? Does your learner remember the main points of the test debrief?

Does your learner have a driving test booked?

CORE OF THE LESSON

The importance of not driving:

- too slow or too fast
- too close to the left/centre of the road

Judgement of the speed and distance of approaching traffic

- Confidence to make progress

Speed

The importance of driving at a speed

- Within the legal limits
- At which the car can be stopped well within the distance seen to be clear
- That suits the prevailing road and traffic conditions

Progress

The importance of:

- sound traffic judgement

This involves the ability to avoid:

- needless hesitancy at junctions or other occasions where it might be safe to proceed

Road position

The importance of:

- a correct safety line
- lane discipline

USEFUL LESSON HINTS:

- Driving faults should be mainly dealt with on the move

- Any debriefs should be used to consolidate the practice

- Watch for your learner going to extremes by being:

  - too slow or fast for particular conditions

  - too close to the left or too close to approaching traffic

- When teaching restraint and the need to hold back, it may be possible to draw on the demonstrations of bad driving provided by other road users. These can often illustrate learning points.

- New learner drivers will tend to drive slowly. Their ability will need to be stretched so that, if on faster roads, they will need to be capable of driving safely with the flow.

- To gain a full licence test candidates must demonstrate competency and drive with confidence and make safe progress. Someone who keeps stopping needlessly at 'Give Way' lines cannot be expected to pass.

- The rule of the road to keep to the left will have been introduced on your learner's very first lesson.. are there any exceptions that still need to be covered?

- On an ADI Part 3 test you can expect to have to teach these topics at Phase 2 only.

PHRASEOLOGY

Adapt your phraseology to suit different road and traffic situations. For example:

"Is it safe to drive at 30mph?"

"What is the danger of being too close to the kerb/approaching traffic?"

SKILLS DEVELOPMENT

The skills to be taught and developed for the learner or qualified driver are that they need to be driving at the correct speed, and be in the correct position for prevailing road and traffic conditions.

Using the driving plan, MSM, all drivers should be trained to get the balance between not going too fast or too slow. It can be as dangerous to drive too slow as it is to drive too fast. Speed choice depends on factors including the legal limit, visibility, road surface conditions and the anticipated actions of other road users as well as the possibility of unseen hazards.

The basic 'rule of the road' is that we drive on the left. Factors that will influence this position include traffic signs, road markings and how the traffic is flowing to accommodate such common features as roadworks, parked vehicles and congestion. We need to ensure that we are in the best road position for the intended route.

The overriding consideration for the use of speed, making progress and road positioning has to be safety.

Instruction Method: Below are some examples of questions that you might ask your learner when they have practised this exercise sufficiently. You should judge the balance of 'telling' and 'Q&A' on how the learner responds to your prompts.

Topic Key Point:	Sample Question:
Speed limits	What is the speed limit on this road?
Road and traffic conditions	Is it safe to drive at the limit?
Hesitancy	What will be the problem if you drive too slowly or hesitate where it is safe to proceed?
Positioning	Where should you normally position the car when driving along?

Typical faults to anticipate

- Driving too fast for the traffic conditions.

- Driving too slowly for the traffic conditions.

- Undue hesitancy, particularly emerging at road junctions including roundabouts.

- Driving too close to the centre of the road.

- Driving too close to the pavement.

- Poor lane discipline.

Finally, as with all driving practise under instruction, complete the instructional core competencies by being sure that your learner knows and understands the causes of any driving faults and the solutions that you have provided.

LESSON XIV: KNOW YOUR TRAFFIC SIGNS, LIGHTS AND ROAD MARKINGS

KEY LEARNING POINTS

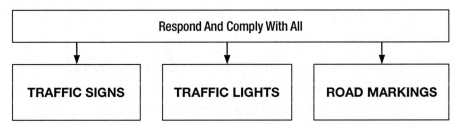

An Approved Driving Instructor must never under-estimate the value of traffic signs, lights and road markings when teaching people to drive. They play an enormous role in regulating traffic flow and behaviour. We know the penalties for disobeying traffic light signals; these also exist for certain traffic signs. Many signs warn road users of hazards and others provide helpful information. Road markings fulfil a very similar role, sometimes in conjunction with traffic signs and lights. Drivers must also be prepared for traffic schemes where traffic signs, lights and road markings are omitted.

STAGE OF ABILITY

- Partly-Trained or Trained

RECAP

- Multiple-Choice Questions used on Theory Test.

- Traffic signs, lights and road markings used at junctions and pedestrian crossings.

CORE OF THE LESSON

- The system of traffic sign shapes and coloured backgrounds and borders.

- Meaning and sequence of traffic light signals.

- Meaning and importance of the most common road markings.

- Recognition and correct responses to all traffic signs, light signals and road markings.

Traffic Signs giving ORDERS

The importance of:

- Complying with the law

- Knowing the difference between mandatory signs and those that indicate a prohibition

- The need to respond to circular signs in plenty of time

Traffic Signs giving WARNINGS

The importance of:

- Being aware of potential dangers

- The need to respond to triangular signs in plenty of time

Traffic Signs giving INFORMATION

The importance of:

- Following route directions and/or advice given

- Knowing the meanings of coloured borders and symbols

- Using these signs during independent driving

Traffic Light Signals

The importance of obeying light signals at:

- Road junctions

- All types of controlled crossings, eg pedestrian; railway (level); fire and/or ambulance stations

- Road works

Road Markings

The importance of obeying or recognising

- 'Give Way' and 'Stop' lines

- Single and double white line systems in the centre of the road

- Coloured reflective studs ('cats eyes')

- Lane lines

- White zig-zag lines at pedestrian crossings

- White hatch markings (chevrons)

- Word markings (eg Slow, Keep Clear, Bus Stop, Turn Right etc)

- Yellow lines (eg restricting waiting and access to box junctions)

- Red lines restricting any stopping at the kerbside

USEFUL LESSON HINTS

- Traffic signs, light signals and road markings convey orders, warnings and information. Avoid presuming that your learner has seen or understand their meanings. Do check.

Spend some time comparing these traffic signs:

'Dual Carriageway Ahead'and 'Road Narrows'

- 'Turn Left' and 'Keep Left'

- 'Steep Hill Upwards' and 'Steep Hill Downwards'

- 'Two way traffic straight ahead' and 'Two way traffic crosses one way road'

- 'Cycle Route Ahead' ,'Cyclist Only', 'No cycling route to be used by pedal cyclists only'

PHRASEOLOGY

Adapt your phraseology to prioritise an important traffic sign. For example:

"How many traffic signs can you see ahead and which is the most important one to prioritise?"

"What does the next sign order to you to do?"

SKILLS DEVELOPMENT

A good way to introduce commentary driving is to ask the learner to identify selected traffic signs and/or road markings and comment how these affect road speed, progress and position.

Advances in technology are used to assist drivers reach their destinations safely. These changes have recently brought about new traffic signs such as:

- Active traffic management

- Advanced stop lines for pedal cyclists

- Vehicle activated signs (Slow Down – 30 mph limit)

- Congestion charging (in London)

- Signs for trams

Instruction Method: Ask your learner, or qualified driver to identify a particular traffic sign or type of road marking. Then ask a question concerning how the warning, order or information might affect their use of speed or road position. Use local traffic signs, varying the route to see which are the most common or unusual signs.

Traffic Sign: **Sample Question:**

Is today a school day and will children be crossing?

How must we respond if we see accompanied horses or ponies?

What will you do if you see a wild animal ahead?

What type of road marking would you expect to accompany this order?

In what type of street would you expect to see this order?

What are the differences in meaning between these two traffic signs?

What type of route sign is this?

What type of route sign is this?

Where would you expect to find this information sign?

Road Marking: **Sample Question:**

What is the difference in meaning between these types of lines that run down the centre of a single carriageway road?

Typical faults to anticipate:

- Failing to see traffic sign or road marking.
- Late response to a foreseeable danger.

Finally, as with all driving practise under instruction, complete the instructional core competencies by being sure that your learner knows and understands the causes of any driving faults and the solutions that you have provided.

LESSON XV: INDEPENDENT DRIVING

KEY LEARNING POINTS

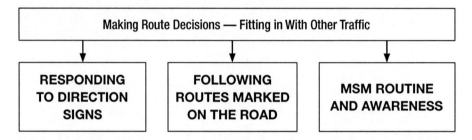

Making Route Decisions — Fitting in With Other Traffic

RESPONDING TO DIRECTION SIGNS	FOLLOWING ROUTES MARKED ON THE ROAD	MSM ROUTINE AND AWARENESS

The object of independent driving is to bridge the gap between learning to drive and driving in the real world and so, create safer drivers. Ever since the driving test was introduced over 75 years ago, one of the biggest challenges for newly qualified driver has been the empty front passenger seat. To help prepare new drivers for this experience, ADIs have, most probably without realising it, been matching route directions to suit the learner's level of driving ability.

STAGE OF ABILITY

• Trained

RECAP

• Using Mirror Signal Manoeuvre (MSM) routine when changing direction

Continue to plan training routes before lessons, using local knowledge to include or avoid certain road and traffic conditions. The route or location must be suited to the lesson topics. These include using the car's controls

correctly; adopting the correct road procedures and developing a responsible attitude to driving.

CORE OF THE LESSON

- Journey and route planning.
- Types of direction signs.
- Identifying primary and non-primary direction signs on the move.
- Following advance verbal directions using a diagram where needed.
- Recognising destination place names.
- Continuing to use the mirrors well before signalling or changing direction.

EFFECTIVE COMMUNICATION

Communicate directions and other relevant information clearly and concisely while the learner is driving, ensuring the complete safety of all road users. The type of route directions, informing a learner when to turn, must match the learner's level of driving ability.

USEFUL LESSON HINTS

- Refer to previous learning and knowledge used on the Theory Test.
- Use the 'Highway Code' and 'Know Your Traffic Signs' to explain types of direction sign.
- Include more detailed general advice on journey planning. This can include brief information on how to avoid known hold-ups at certain times of the day as well as the use of SatNav systems.
- Give conventional directions to turn where the learner experiences any difficulty or requests help.
- Where a learner is likely to forget the directions do not overload them with a complex route.
- Watch out for those with weak spatial awareness or lack of recognition of left and right – they may need to be told to go "your way" or "my

way"; ask the person how they learn best and follow their effective methods for them.

- To help an individual memorise something, get them to suggest a memory peg such as a rhyme or a picture they can visualise or something very zany; all this helps make the memory more memorable!

USEFUL DRIVING TEST HINTS

- Since 4 October 2010 the practical driving test has included a short section of independent driving.

- During the test candidates have to drive by either following traffic signs, a series of directions, or a combination of both, for about ten minutes.

- Where candidates are asked to follow a series of verbal directions, they'll be shown a diagram to help.

- It doesn't matter if they don't remember every direction, or if they go the wrong way – that can happen to the most experienced drivers. It won't affect the result of your test unless they commit a driving fault.

- Independent driving is not a test of orientation and navigation skills. Driving independently means making sensible decisions – this includes deciding when it's safe and appropriate to ask for confirmation about where to go.

- If there are poor or obscured traffic signs, the examiner will give directions until the next traffic sign can be seen – candidates won't need to have a detailed knowledge of the area.

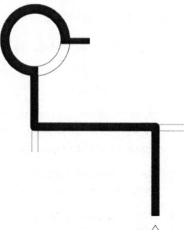

- If the candidate goes off the route or takes a wrong turning, the examiner will help them to get back on the route and continue with the independent driving exercise.

- If a special need is involved, no more than three directions will be issued at one time and this may be shortened to two. DSA can identify any special needs and disabilities

when tests are booked online or over the phone, so that reasonable adjustment can be made for the candidate.

- Where a candidate has some form of dyslexia, examiners will ask the person what adjustments they need. For instance, their preference for verbal directions or to following signs. Diagrams are reproduced on cream vellum paper which cuts down on visual distraction. If helpful, visual clues to the diagram may be added, such as a supermarket or petrol station on route, or telling the candidate the number of the exit point on roundabouts (for example, "It's the third exit"). Landmarks may be used such as "Take the first left, it's just past the cinema". Directions can be adapted from saying right and left to "Your side", "My side".

- Where a candidate speaks little or no English the examiner will write place names so that it is clear to you where they are being asked to drive to. ADIs can now act as interpreters on driving tests.

PHRASEOLOGY

"Follow the direction signs for the town centre."

"From my diagram, follow this route … at the end of this road turn left, then … etc."

Adapt the route directions to suit your geographic location.

SKILLS DEVELOPMENT

Introduce the skill to drive on directions gradually, for instance beginning with a single direction with a destination, for example "Take the next road on the right, following the route towards the town centre …. thank you".

Gradually increase the number of verbal directions given, or route signs to follow, to run over longer periods of time, ensuring that they are competent to concentrate on these for a minimum of ten minutes.

Instruction Method: Below are some examples of questions that you might ask your learner when they have practised sufficiently. Any questions used must be appropriate to the learner and the circumstances of the lesson. Judge the balance of 'telling' and 'Q&A' on how the learner responds to your guidance.

Topic Key Point:	Sample Question:
Destination place name	According to the next direction sign, which way do we need to turn to get to the town centre?
	Thank You. In that case, take the next road on the left/right or at the end of the road turn left/right towards the town centre.
Route map	According to the map which way do we need to turn next?

Typical faults to anticipate:

- Not seeing the direction sign.

- Seeing the direction sign late.

- Misinterpreting the direction sign.

- Forgetting the place name or series of directions.

- Not using the MSM routine correctly.

Finally, as with all driving practise under instruction, complete the instructional core competencies by being sure that your learner knows and understands the causes of any driving faults and the solutions that you have provided.

LESSON XVI: REVERSING INTO AN OPENING

KEY LEARNING POINTS

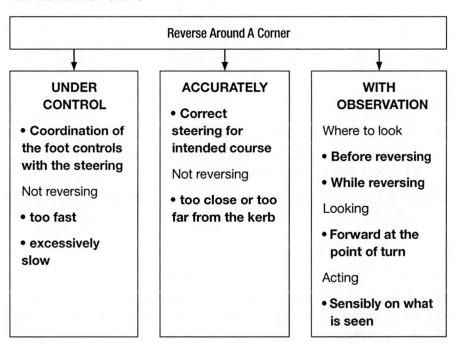

Reverse Around A Corner		
UNDER CONTROL	**ACCURATELY**	**WITH OBSERVATION**
• **Coordination of the foot controls with the steering**	• **Correct steering for intended course**	Where to look
Not reversing	Not reversing	• **Before reversing**
• **too fast**	• **too close or too far from the kerb**	• **While reversing**
• **excessively slow**		Looking
		• **Forward at the point of turn**
		Acting
		• **Sensibly on what is seen**

Reversing, is a very useful skill that helps us if we need to change our travel direction. It is also necessary when parking in a car park, or at the roadside.

The number of minor collisions caused by qualified drivers when reverse manoeuvring is significant. These, however result in relatively few serious injuries or fatalities. To avoid costly repairs, the newly qualified driver often has to accurately adapt their reversing skills to a different vehicle. This involves adapting any techniques taught on lessons, such as the use of reference and focal points.

When reversing, drivers must only turn the steering wheel while the vehicle is moving. Other hand-holds on the steering wheel may well make manoeuvres easier, especially in a confined space.

STAGE OF ABILITY

- Partly-Trained

RECAP

- The Preparation Observation Manoeuvre (POM) routine, clutch and brake control

Most of the skills to reverse safely should already have been learnt whilst driving forwards.

For instance:

- POM routine when moving off at the start of the reverse.

- The manoeuvring skills involving use of the clutch and gas pedal or just the brake pedal in coordination with the steering.

All your learner needs to do now are the same things using reverse gear.

CORE OF THE LESSON

Why is reversing part of the learning to drive syllabus?

We do need to drive backwards, albeit only a short distance. We may have to turn back and go the opposite way, this becomes easier and it's much more efficient if you are good at reversing.

How will you:

- know that your learner is ready for this exercise?

- link previous knowledge to this exercise?

Which site will you use?

Choose somewhere quiet and flat where you can begin with a straight reverse before going around a corner.

On approach to the corner:

- use the MSM routine.

Why is it important:

- to get your learner to turn in the seat so as to see properly through the rear window?

- for you to also turn in your seat so as to see properly through the rear window?

- Will you or your learner need to remove your seat belts?

A system of instruction

The importance of EDP:

- Explanation – using the 'Question and Answer' technique

- Demonstration – will this help? Is a diagram enough?

- Practise – Talk your learner through the exercise

A system of approach

The importance of:

- using the POM/MSM routines

- instructing in stages

Control

The importance of:

- coordinating the foot controls with the steering

- not reversing too fast or too slow

Accuracy

The importance of:

- keeping reasonably close to the kerb

- using focal and reference points

Observation

The importance of:

- observation before starting to reverse

- observation before and during the reverse

- observation at the point of turn

- giving way to other drivers, cyclists and pedestrians where necessary

---

THE LEFT REVERSE

Three easy stages

Before moving away and pulling up beyond the corner to start the exercise:

Remember:

- the MSM routine

- to look into the junction

1. Straight reverse

- POM Routine

- Control and accuracy
  The car should be about 45cm (18 inches from the kerb). Take note of the car's position through the rear window.

- Use a focal point at the bottom of the rear window that suits the learner's height and driving position.

- Observation
  Mainly over the left shoulder to achieve rear vision, but including glances forward, to the sides and in the mirrors.

  Reverse very slowly, keeping the car parallel with the kerb. Pull up just before the rear nearside wheel reaches the point of turn. Use a reference point outside the car such as a point on one of the kerbstones.

2. The corner

*   POM
    The general rule is to follow the kerb as it disappears from view in the rear window and reappears in the nearside rear window.

*   Control and accuracy
    At the point of turn, the amount of steering to the left needed depends on how sharp the corner is.

*   Observation
    Look in the direction of travel. Do keep checking ahead and in the blindspots.

    If another road user approaches on the main road, a decision to pause or continue has to be made. It can sometimes be better to keep moving and clear the junction, rather than becoming an obstruction by waiting.

3. Straight reverse

*   Control and accuracy
    How to straighten the car up (using the focal point) and keep a reasonable distance from the kerb. How far to travel back.

*   Observation
    Over the left shoulder with glances forwards and to the sides. If another driver appears to the rear, consider the necessary action which will minimize any inconvenience or potential danger. It may be necessary to pull forwards round the corner to allow the vehicle to pass.

    Given the change in vehicle design in recent years, car rear windows are becoming smaller in order to increase passenger cell strength. Observation when reversing should be 'all round and effective'. Be sure that any prioritising suggested in the advice here, does not lead to a form of tunnel vision.

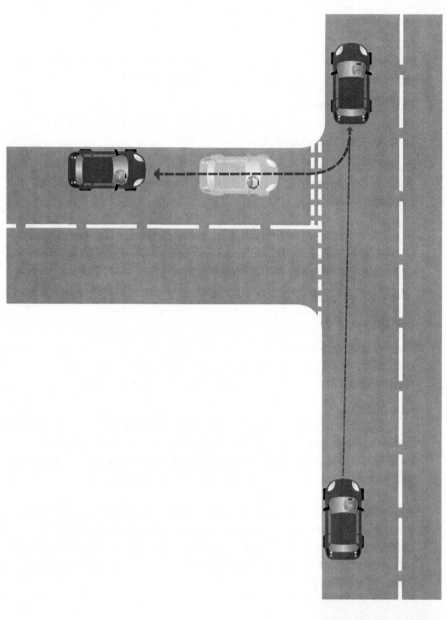

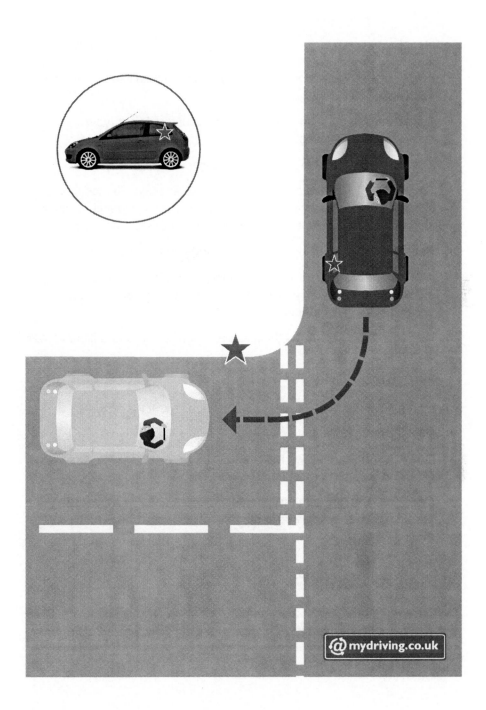

USEFUL LESSON HINTS:

- Always use an illustration. If the one you have doesn't suit the corner you've chosen – draw your own.

- Talk yourself through your own reversing round different types of corners before teaching.

- Never reverse from a minor road to a major road or at a crossroads.

- Focal points inside the car can help achieve an accurate manoeuvre. It shouldn't be necessary to use in-car markers such as matchsticks or sticky labels to denote a focal point in the rear or side windows.

- Reference points outside the car help judgement of the car's position.

- With modern cars it is usually necessary to use the mirrors as an aid when reversing, so glances, such as in the nearside mirror, are necessary and acceptable.

- Vary your choice of site as the lessons progress. Choose different types of corners:

  - sharp 90° corners

  - gradual corners

- Use different gradients.

- Observe your learner. You may need to sit sideways to face your learner. On a Part 3 test you must keep your belt on.

- Once you're happy with your learner's performance when reversing to the left, go on to teach a right-hand reverse. Explain why you are doing this.

PHRASEOLOGY – REVERSING

The following phraseology is an example of what you might need to say. Don't assume that this is all you have to say or exactly what you will need to say every time. Your learner may not do what you ask, so you may have to repeat a particular phrase in a different way.

AN ALTERNATIVE EXAMPLE OF INSTRUCTIONAL GUIDANCE / COMMENTARY FOR LEFT CORNER REVERSE

Pull over and park on the left just before the corner you want to reverse around. Prepare to move off in first gear, look around for any road users or pedestrians, and drive slowly forwards past the junction. As you do so have a good look into the road to make sure there are no obstacles preventing you from carrying out the manoeuvre. And look at the curve of the corner: is it gentle or sharp?

Brake when the car is roughly 2 car lengths past the corner. Depending on the width of the road, you should be no more than about half a metre away from the kerb. Don't forget to apply the handbrake.

If you find it difficult to look over your shoulder with your seat belt on, you can take it off for the duration of the manoeuvre.

Put the gear into reverse and find the biting point, if you need to.

Have a good look all around, including in the mirrors. If it is safe to move, release the handbrake, look over your left shoulder and gradually raise the clutch. Keep the speed of the car slow and steady as you move backwards using clutch control.

Make a note of the point where the kerb cuts the bottom of the rear windscreen. Keep this focal point in mind for later.

Your point of turn depends somewhat on your height in the car but can usually be judged as when the straight kerb stones in the side road appear in the rear side window.

Before steering, look all around the outside of the car, then steer left to take the car round the corner. Reverse into the turn, looking into the side road, but also checking for other traffic.

Keep your speed down to stay in control. Check how close you are to the kerb by glancing in the left door mirror occasionally.

Look for the original focal point, when the line of the kerb stones gets close to it, steer right to straighten your car parallel with the kerb.

Continue reversing down the road a short distance at a steady pace. Don't forget to glance frequently out of the front of the car, as another vehicle may well have turned into the road after you.

When you have reversed far enough back, brake gently, apply the handbrake and move the gears back to neutral. If you did remove your seat belt, don't forget to put it back on.

SKILLS DEVELOPMENT

Reversing in a straight line, then around different types of left and right corners, is our normal introduction to the set-piece exercises. These exercises are part of learning the size, shape and manoeuvrability of the vehicle.

Success with this series of manoeuvres requires the demonstration of three essential skills:

1. Vehicle control: coordinating the foot controls and steering.

2. Accuracy: following the curve of the kerb, be it sharp or gentle.

3. Observation: being aware of any traffic, including pedestrians.

Eco-safe tip: Always perform your manoeuvres with a warm engine; it's much more eco-friendly.

Instruction Method: Use a diagram to explain each exercise and offer a demonstration. Below are some examples of questions that you might ask your learner. With experience you can devise your own bank of possible questions. Questions used must be appropriate to the learner and the circumstances of the lesson. Judge the balance of 'telling' and 'Q&A' on how the learner responds to your guidance.

Topic Key Point:	Sample Question:
Recap at beginning	Have you reversed a car before?
Type of corner	Is the corner sharp or gradual?
Gradient	Is the road flat?
Straight reverse	What can you remember about reversing in a straight line?
Starting the exercise	How far beyond the corner will you need to be to start the exercise?

Reference points	At what point will you begin to steer round the corner and when will you need to straighten the vehicle up?
Focal points	How will you judge your distance from the corner?
Finishing the exercise	How far past the corner into the road should you reverse?

Typical faults to anticipate

- Control – too fast (or too slow).
- Accuracy – too wide or hitting/scraping kerb.
- Observation – not looking in direction of travel.
- Not looking ahead at the point of turn.
- Not checking blind spot before steering.
- Not making necessary all round observation.
- Including glances to the front and the appropriate mirrors.
- Not showing proper recognition of other road users.

Finally, as with all driving practise under instruction, complete the instructional core competencies by being sure that your learner knows and understands the causes of any driving faults and the solutions that you have provided.

LESSON XVII: RIGHT CORNER REVERSE

The Right Corner Reverse is a mandatory exercise on the ADI Part 2 qualifying examination. Also, new drivers who take a driving test in a van or estate car may be asked to reverse round a right-hand corner.

The exercise should be taught to all new drivers, although it is often omitted.

STAGE OF ABILITY

- Partly-Trained (For ADI PST purposes)

RECAP

- Left Corner Reverse

The skills to reverse safely around a left corner (POM routine, coordination of all the controls along with all round observations) can be transferred to this exercise.

CORE OF THE LESSON

Why do we need to reverse around a right-hand corner?

As well as providing an extra means to be able to turn back, it is a safer way to manoeuvre a van or other vehicle with limited/poor side or rear vision.

Pre-drawn diagrams are commercially available or can be improvised. These will help to make it clear what you expect your driver to do. As with the left reverse, it's better to introduce the exercise in stages.

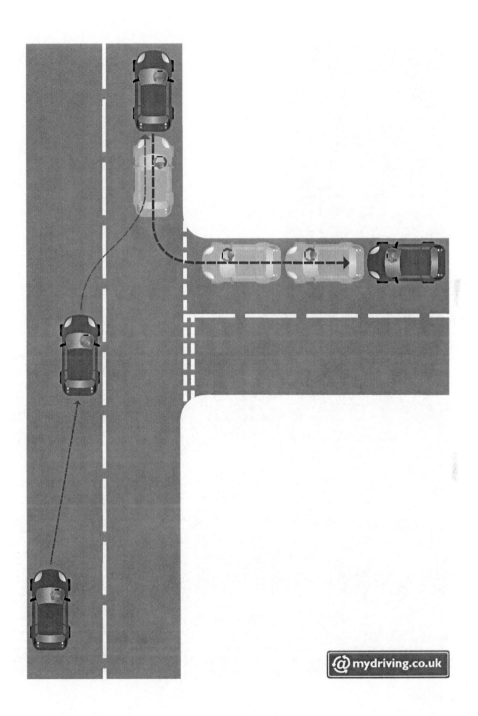

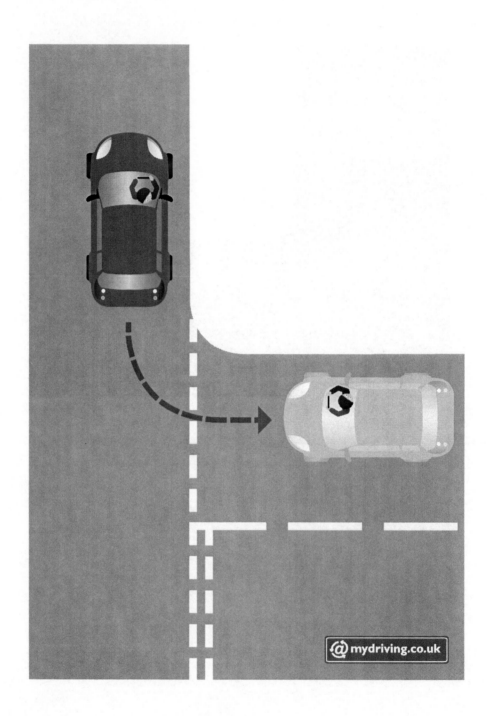

Appendix 2   Lesson plans and diagrams   199

1. Moving off and pulling up beyond the corner to start the exercise.

Remember

- The MSM Routine.

- To look into the junction (to make sure there is enough room to complete the exercise safely).

- Pull up immediately beyond the junction and reasonably close to the offside kerb.

2. Straight reverse

- POM Routine.

- Control and accuracy
  Move the vehicle back slowly, keeping it reasonably close to the kerb. To ensure accuracy it is acceptable to use the offside mirror. The driver should also look over the right shoulder and if necessary, wind the window down. Keep a close check on how close the car is to the kerb and the corner. Pull up before the offside rear wheel reaches the point of turn. If necessary, use a suitable reference point outside the car.

- Observation
  As well as following the kerb, the driver must also glance ahead frequently and in the left door mirror. In a car, the observation needs to be mainly in the direction of travel. Keep looking all round and respond sensibly to any approaching traffic.

3. The corner

- POM Routine

- Control and accuracy
  The amount of steering and how quickly this needs to be, depends on how sharp or gentle the corner is.

- Observation
  Before steering, look all around and then over the right shoulder, through the offside window. Do keep looking all round. While reversing, keep checking ahead, making glances in the door mirrors as well as over to the left in a car. If another driver approaches on the main road, judge whether you can keep moving or need to wait while the driver passes.

4. Straight reverse

-   Control and accuracy
    Straighten the steering so that the car is parallel with the kerb, keep
    it a reasonable distance from the kerb. Not too far and not too close.
    As the car is on the opposite side of the road, it is safer to travel back
    a greater distance before finishing the manoeuvre. This will minimize
    danger from other vehicles turning into the junction.

-   Observation
    As soon as the car becomes parallel with the kerb, resume all round
    observation. Focus on the direction of travel, glancing ahead and in the
    left door mirror as well. During this manoeuvre, where another road user
    appears to be close, or is likely to get close, consider the necessary
    action that will minimize any inconvenience or potential danger.

A system of instruction

The importance of EDP:

-   Explanation – using the 'Question and Answer' technique

-   Demonstration – will this help? Is a diagram enough?

-   Practise – Talk your learner through the exercise

A system of approach

The importance of:

-   using the POM/MSM routines

-   instructing in stages

Control

The importance of:

-   coordinating the foot controls with the steering

-   not reversing too fast or too slow

Accuracy

The importance of:

- keeping reasonably close to the kerb

- using focal and reference points

Observation

The importance of:

- observation before starting to reverse

- observation before and during the reverse

- observation at the point of turn

- giving way to other drivers, cyclists and pedestrians where necessary

USEFUL LESSON HINTS:

- Always use an illustration! If the one you have doesn't suit the right corner you've chosen – draw your own!

- Talk yourself through your own reversing round different types of right corners.

- Never reverse:

    - From a minor road to a major road

    - At a crossroads

- Focal points inside the car can help achieve an accurate manoeuvre. It shouldn't be necessary to use in-car markers such as matchsticks or sticky labels to denote a focal point in the rear or side windows.

- Reference points outside the car help judgement of the car's position.

- With modern cars it is usually necessary to use the mirrors as an aid when reversing, so glances, such as in the nearside and offside mirrors, are necessary and acceptable.

- Vary your choice of site as the lessons progress. Choose different types of corners:

    - sharp 90° corners

    - gradual corners

- Use different gradients.

- Observe your learner – you may need to sit sideways to face your learner, but on an ADI Part Three test you must keep your seat belt on.

PHRASEOLOGY

Adapt the phraseology used when introducing straight reversing and teaching the left corner reverse.

SKILLS DEVELOPMENT

Reversing successfully round different types of corner is part of learning the size, shape and manoeuvrability of the vehicle.

Successful manoeuvring requires the demonstration of three essential skills:

1. Vehicle control: coordinating the foot controls and steering.

2. Accuracy: following the curve of the kerb, be it sharp or gentle.

3. Observation: being aware of any traffic, including pedestrians.

Eco-safe tip: Always perform your manoeuvres with a warm engine; it's much more eco-friendly.

Instruction Method: Use a diagram to explain each exercise and offer a demonstration. Below are some examples of questions that you might ask your learner. With experience you can devise your own bank of possible questions. Questions used must be appropriate to the learner and the circumstances of the lesson. Judge the balance of 'telling' and 'Q&A' on how the learner responds to your guidance.

Topic Key Point:	Sample Question:
Recap at beginning	What are the skills needed to reverse round a corner?
Type of corner	Is the corner sharp or gradual?
Gradient	Is the road flat?
Starting the exercise	How far beyond the corner will you need to be to start the exercise?
Straight reverse	Where will you need to look when reversing in a straight line?
Reference points	At what point will you begin to steer round the corner and when will you need to straighten the vehicle up?
Focal points	How will you judge your distance from the corner?
Finishing the exercise	How far passed the corner into the road should you reverse?

Typical faults to anticipate

- Control – too fast (or too slow).
- Accuracy – too wide or hitting/scraping kerb.
- Observation – not looking in direction of travel.
- Not looking ahead at the point of turn.
- Not checking blind spot before steering.
- Not making necessary all round observation, including glances to the front and the appropriate mirrors.
- Not showing proper recognition of other road users.

Finally, as with all driving practise under instruction, complete the instructional core competencies by being sure that your learner knows and understands the causes of any driving faults and the solutions that you have provided.

LESSON XVIII: REVERSE PARKING

KEY LEARNING POINTS

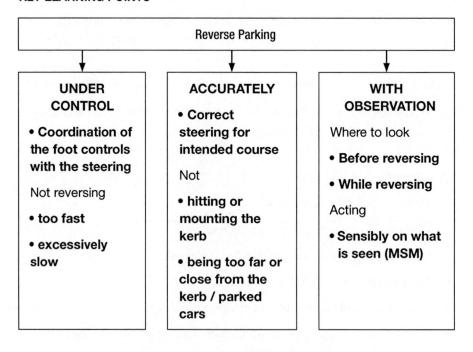

Reverse Parking		
UNDER CONTROL • **Coordination of the foot controls with the steering** Not reversing • **too fast** • **excessively slow**	**ACCURATELY** • **Correct steering for intended course** Not • **hitting or mounting the kerb** • **being too far or close from the kerb / parked cars**	**WITH OBSERVATION** Where to look • **Before reversing** • **While reversing** Acting • **Sensibly on what is seen (MSM)**

Prior to the introduction of the Reverse Parking exercise into the driving test, instructors knew the exercise as 'Parallel Parking' where learners were taught how to park between two other cars.

Reverse, or parallel parking makes use of the vehicle's manoeuvrability in reverse gear. To prevent damage to the vehicle, drivers must however avoid any temptation to turn the steering wheel while the vehicle is stationary.

STAGE OF ABILITY

- Trained

RECAP

- Reversing exercises

CORE OF THE LESSON

Why is reverse parking part of the 'Learning to Drive' training course?

Reverse parking enables drivers to make use of parking spaces that cannot be driven into. How will you:

- know that your learner is ready for this exercise?
- link previous knowledge to the reverse park exercise?

POM/MSM routine

Ability to combine safe observation with good coordination of all the car's controls.

Which site will you use?

Choose somewhere quiet. You need only one parked car (reverse parking) to practise this exercise.

When your learner shows competence, go on to use two cars parked no less than two car lengths apart (parallel parking).

A system of instruction

The importance of EDP:

- Explanation – using the 'Question and Answer' technique
- Demonstration – will this help? Is a diagram enough?
- Practice – Talk your learner through the exercise

A system of approach

The importance of:

- using the POM/MSM routines
- instructing in stages

Control

The importance of:

- coordinating the foot controls with the steering
- not reversing too fast or too slow

Accuracy

The importance of completing the exercise:

- within two car lengths from the parked vehicle in front
- parallel with the kerb

The importance of:

- not being too close to any parked vehicle
- not being too close or too far from the kerb
- sight lines (s)

Observation

The importance of:

- observation before starting to reverse
- observation before and during the reverse
- observation at the point of turn
- giving way to other drivers, cyclists and pedestrians where necessary

REVERSE PARKING BEHIND ONE PARKED CAR

Four easy stages

- Before moving away and pulling up alongside the parked car to start the exercise, remember to make sure there is no traffic around.

- Use the MSM routine.

1. Starting to reverse

- Begin in a straight position, level with, and no more than a metre (approximately 3 feet) from the lead stationary vehicle.

- POM

Preparation: Select reverse gear as part of the preparation.

- Observation
  The reversing lights will inform drivers that approach from the rear of your learner's intention. Advise your learner to signal left if it will help another driver. Consider use of the brake lights to confirm that you are waiting for any vehicle to pass if safe.

  After the normal observations watch to make sure that your learner looks mainly over the left shoulder to the rear and includes forward glances.

2. Starting to steer left

- Manoeuvre (accuracy and control)
  When the rear of the training car is level with the rear of the stationary vehicle start to steer left (keep the car moving slowly).

3. Steering to the right

- When the training car is nearly half way in (gauge its steering wheel with the rear of the lead stationary vehicle) steer quite briskly to the right.

- Observation
  Check the danger of clipping the stationary lead vehicle.

  Glances in the nearside mirror are permitted, but should not be at the expense of looking to the side or through the rear window.

  Use a sight line with the offside of the lead stationary vehicle to assist accuracy.

4. Straightening the steering wheels

- As the training car comes close to the kerb, steer left and finish with the wheels straight.

PARALLEL PARKING BETWEEN TWO PARKED CARS

- Always practise parking behind one parked car first!

- You will need a parking space of at least one and a half times the length of your training car to do this second manoeuvre.

- Adapt the method for reverse parking behind one parked car.

- To help judge when the training car is half way in, the offside of the training car should be lined up with the nearside headlamp of stationary car behind your parking space.

- Don"t allow the rear nearside tyres to touch the kerb or be too far out. Instead it is better to move forwards and then backwards again to correct any error or straighten the training car up.

USEFUL LESSON HINTS:

- Use an illustration.

- Talk yourself through your own reversing.

- Focal points inside the car can help achieve an accurate manoeuvre. It shouldn't be necessary to use in-car markers such as matchsticks or sticky labels to denote a focal point in the rear or side windows.

- Reference points / Site line (s) outside the car help judgement of the car's position.

- With modern cars it is usually necessary to use the mirrors as an aid when reversing, so glances, such as in the nearside mirror, are necessary and acceptable.

- Observe your learner. You may need to sit sideways to face your learner. On a Part 3 test you must keep your belt on.

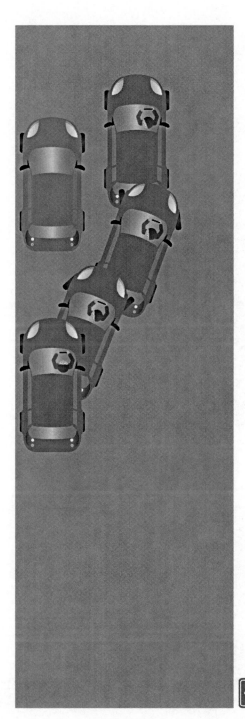

how2become

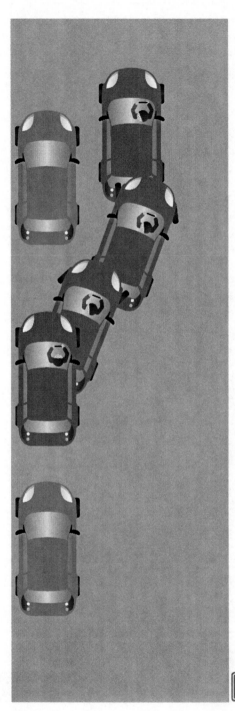

PHRASEOLOGY – REVERSE PARKING

This is an example of guidance/commentary. You will need to adapt it to suit your learner, the vehicle and the circumstances where you are teaching this exercise.

Drive forward past the empty space and use the footbrake to stop parallel to the car on your left hand side. Don't stop more than a metre from the car as you may cause greater obstruction than necessary.

Press your foot down on the clutch and select reverse gear, then lightly press down on the accelerator and raise the clutch close to the biting point.

Check all around for other road users, look over your left shoulder through the rear window, if the way is clear, drive back very slowly.

Watch for the rear corner of the car to your left in your rear side window. When you can see it, check all around and if safe turn the steering wheel to the left one full turn. Check the road both ways and then continue reversing very slowly at an angle into the space. When the front of your car is aligned with the rear bumper of the car in front, turn the steering wheel fully to the right, which will swing your car in towards the kerb.

Using clutch and brake controls slow the car right down, straighten the steering a little as you do so. You should be close to the kerb, but if not, you can move forwards and backwards to get it right. You will get a feel for how close you should be the more you practise.

Avoid letting your tyres touch the kerb. And don't steer whilst stationary, as this is bad for your tyres and steering.

SKILLS DEVELOPMENT

Reverse parking is an essential practical skill in today's traffic conditions. Being able to carry this exercise out successfully demonstrates that the driver is totally familiar with the size and positioning of the vehicle. Success with this manoeuvre requires the demonstration of three essential skills:

1. Vehicle control: coordinating the foot controls and steering.
2. Accuracy: knowing when and how much to steer to park the car.
3. Observation: being aware of any traffic, including pedestrians.

Parking a car isn't difficult to master. It just needs enough practise using some simple techniques.

Eco-safe tip: Always perform your manoeuvres with a warm engine; it's much more eco-friendly!

Instruction Method: Use a diagram to explain each exercise and offer a demonstration. Below are some examples of questions that you might ask your learner. With experience you can devise your own bank of possible questions. Questions used must be appropriate to the learner and the circumstances of the lesson. Judge the balance of 'telling' and 'Q&A' on how the learner responds to your guidance.

Topic Key Point:	Sample Question:
Site	Where should you not park your vehicle?
Parking on the street and amount of gap between other vehicles	When will you have to parallel park and how much space will you need?
Transferred learning	When you were taught to reverse around a corner and turn in the road, what were the three main aspects of both these exercises?
Illustration	Have you seen this diagram before?
First position and preparation	What routine should you use to move into the first position and how far should you be from the parked car?
Observation	Before beginning to manoeuvre, where must you look?
Manoeuvre into final position	Where should you be looking during the manoeuvre?
	What reference points could you use to help achieve an accurate manoeuvre?
	How will you control the car's speed and how much will you need to steer?

Typical faults to anticipate

- Not positioning level at the correct distance.

- Indecision regarding approaching traffic.

- Inadequate observations and steering.

- Hurrying the exercise and/or not completing the exercise within two car lengths of the parked car.

Finally, as with all driving practise under instruction, complete the instructional core competencies by being sure that your learner knows and understands the causes of any driving faults and the solutions that you have provided.

LESSON XIX: BAY PARKING

KEY LEARNING POINTS

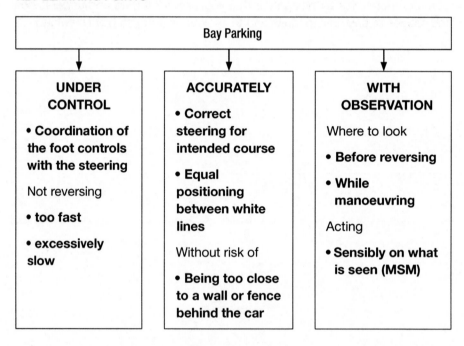

Bay Parking		
UNDER CONTROL	**ACCURATELY**	**WITH OBSERVATION**
• Coordination of the foot controls with the steering	• Correct steering for intended course	Where to look
Not reversing	• Equal positioning between white lines	• Before reversing
• too fast		• While manoeuvring
• excessively slow	Without risk of	Acting
	• Being too close to a wall or fence behind the car	• Sensibly on what is seen (MSM)

Getting to your destination calls for many driving skills. Bay parking is an essential practical skill at the end of any journey and can be assessed at the start or end of a driving test where the Test Centre has parking bays. If you are parking in a car park, or possibly a garage, you will need to know how to reverse into a bay.

As with reverse parking behind a car, this exercise makes use of the vehicle's improved manoeuvrability in reverse gear.

Many instructors make it a routine to teach bay parking beginning straight, then reversing into the bay at 90 degrees. There are advantages to be considered, where there is enough room, to start the exercise at a 45 degree position, which is a common practice amongst most qualified drivers.

STAGE OF ABILITY

- Trained

RECAP

- Reverse Parking

All the skills required to bay park have been learnt whilst reverse parking.

CORE OF THE LESSON

Why is bay parking part of the 'Learning to Drive' training course?

Bay parking in car parks is an essential driving skill.

How will you:

- know that your learner is ready for this exercise?

- link previous knowledge to the bay park exercise?

POM/MSM routine

- Ability to combine safe observation with good coordination of all the car's controls.

- Which site will you use?

Choose somewhere quiet where you won't inconvenience others. You will need to gain permission for the use of private car parks.

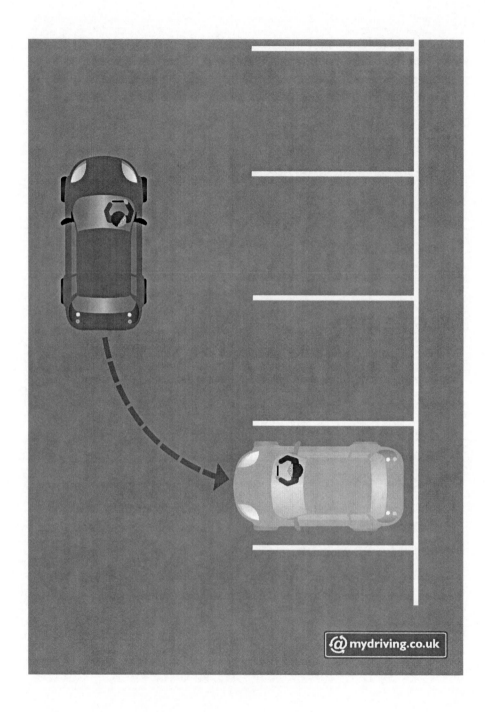

A system of instruction

The importance of EDP:

- Explanation – using the 'Question and Answer' technique
- Demonstration – will this help? Is a diagram enough?
- Practise – Talk your learner through the exercise.

A system of approach

The importance of:

- using the POM/MSM routines
- instructing in stages

Control

The importance of:

- coordinating the foot controls with the steering
- not reversing too fast or too slow

Accuracy

The importance of completing the exercise:

- square between the lines in one bay

Observation

The importance of:

- observation before starting to manoeuvre
- observation during the manoeuvre
- giving way to other drivers, cyclists and pedestrians where necessary

USEFUL LESSON HINTS:

- Use an illustration.
- Consider how you bay park your car.

- When do you start to steer left/right and by how much?

- Where do you look before and whilst steering.

- What are the focal and reference points.

- How will you park square between the lines in one space?

PHRASEOLOGY – BAY PARKING

This is an example of guidance/commentary. You will need to adapt it to suit your learner, the vehicle and the circumstances where you are teaching this exercise.

Drive past the bay in the direction of the road until the rear of your car is aligned with the space. Select reverse gear, check all around, including your blind spot, for obstructions and pedestrians. Then turn your steering wheel in the direction of the bay, reversing very slowly into the space. Keep looking all around as you reverse as well as glancing in your mirrors to check your position and straighten the steering. Park as neatly as possible in the centre of the bay, ensuring that you and your passengers are able to open the doors safely. Secure your car by applying the handbrake and select neutral.

SKILLS DEVELOPMENT

Bay parking is an essential practical skill. Being able to carry this exercise out successfully demonstrates that the driver is totally familiar with the size and positioning of the vehicle. As with the other manoeuvres, success with this manoeuvre requires the demonstration of three essential skills:

1. Vehicle control: coordinating the foot controls and steering.

2. Accuracy: knowing when and how much to steer to park the car.

3. Observation: being aware of any traffic, including pedestrians.

Bay parking a car isn't difficult to master. It just needs enough practise using some simple techniques.

Eco-safe tip: Always perform your manoeuvres with a warm engine; it's much more eco-friendly!

Instruction Method: Use a diagram to explain each exercise and offer a demonstration. Below are some examples of questions that you might ask

your learner. With experience you can devise your own bank of possible questions. Questions used must be appropriate to the learner and the circumstances of the lesson. Judge the balance of 'telling' and 'Q&A' on how the learner responds to your guidance.

Topic Key Point:	Sample Question:
Site	Where should you not park your vehicle?
Transferred learning	When you were taught the reverse manoeuvres, what were the three main aspects of both these exercises?
Illustration	Have you seen this diagram before?
First position and preparation	What routine should you use to move into the first position and where should you position?
Observation	Before beginning to manoeuvre, where must you look?
Manoeuvre into final position	Where should you be looking during the manoeuvre?
	How will you control the car's speed and how much will you need to steer?

Typical faults to anticipate

- Indecision regarding approaching traffic.

- Inadequate observations and steering.

- Hurrying the exercise and/or not completing the exercise square between the lines in one space.

Finally, as with all driving practise under instruction, complete the instructional core competencies by being sure that your learner knows and understands the causes of any driving faults and the solutions that you have provided.

LESSON XX: TURN IN THE ROAD

KEY LEARNING POINTS

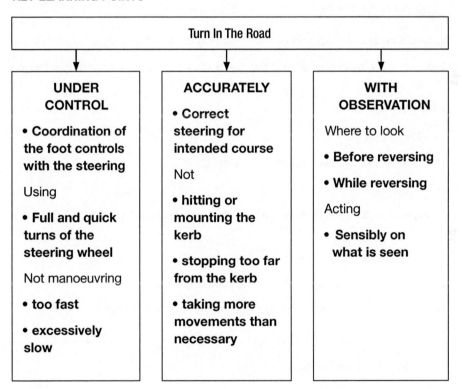

Turn In The Road

UNDER CONTROL

• Coordination of the foot controls with the steering

Using

• Full and quick turns of the steering wheel

Not manoeuvring

• too fast

• excessively slow

ACCURATELY

• Correct steering for intended course

Not

• hitting or mounting the kerb

• stopping too far from the kerb

• taking more movements than necessary

WITH OBSERVATION

Where to look

• Before reversing

• While reversing

Acting

• Sensibly on what is seen

The idea of the turn on the road exercise is to manoeuvre the car so that it faces the opposite direction using forward and reverse gears.

This exercise demonstrates the driver's ability to fully control a car and at the same time look in the right places.

STAGE OF ABILITY

- Partly-Trained

RECAP

- Reversing and manoeuvring

All the skills required to turn the car in the road have been learnt whilst reversing around different types of corner and manoeuvring the car forwards.

CORE OF THE LESSON

Why is turn in the road part of the 'Learning to Drive' training course?

The turn in the road is an alternative method of changing direction to reversing round a corner.

How will you:

- know that your learner is ready for this exercise?
- link previous knowledge to this exercise?

POM routine

Ability to combine safe observation with good coordination of all the car's controls.

- Which site will you use?

Choose somewhere quiet with a slight camber.

- Will you or your learner need to remove your seat belt(s)?

A system of instruction

The importance of EDP:

- Explanation – using the 'Question and Answer' technique .
- Demonstration – will this help? Is a diagram enough?
- Practise – Talk your learner through the exercise.

A system of approach

The importance of:

- using the POM/MSM routines

- instructing in stages

Control

The importance of:

- coordinating the foot controls with the steering

- not reversing too fast or too slow

Accuracy

The importance of:

- completing the turn in as few movements as possible

Observation

The importance of:

- observation before starting to manoeuvre

- observation during the reverse

- giving way to other drivers, cyclists and pedestrians where necessary

- not overhanging the kerb, if this will cause inconvenience to passing pedestrians

USEFUL LESSON HINTS

- Always use an illustration! If the one you have doesn't suit – draw your own!

- Talk yourself through the exercise.

- Observe your learner. You may need to sit sideways to face your learner. On an ADI Part Three test you must keep your seat belt on.

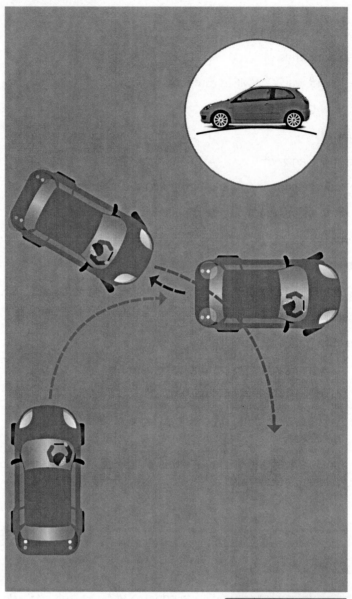

PHRASEOLOGY – TURN IN THE ROAD

The following phraseology is an example of what you might need to say. Don't assume that this is all you have to say or exactly what you will need to say every time. Your learner may not do what you ask, so you may have to repeat a particular phrase in a different way.

For moving away...

- Preparation   Pre-starting checks and start engine

                             Select first gear

-                            Set gas Observation   Normal
  observations

- Manoeuvre   Prepare and release the handbrake
                             (if not already done so)

                             Slowly clutch up until the car moves

                             Feet still

- Exercise   Move slowly forwards using clutch control

                             Steer briskly and fully to the right

                             Over the crown, clutch down and cover
                             brake

                             Steer briskly to the left

                             Move slowly forwards using brake control

                             Gently brake to a stop close to the kerb

                             Apply handbrake. Make the car safe.

For reversing...

- Preparation   Prepare for an uphill start in reverse gear

- Observation   Normal observations

                             First looking over the left shoulder

- Manoeuvre   Prepare and release the handbrake
                             (if not already done so)

                             Slowly clutch up until the car moves

		Feet still
•	Exercise	Move slowly backwards using clutch control
		Steer briskly and fully to the left
		Over the crown, clutch down
		Look over the right shoulder
		Steer briskly to the right
		Move slowly backwards using brake control
		Gently brake to a stop close to the kerb
		Apply handbrake. Make the car safe.

For moving forwards into a parking position...

•	Preparation	Prepare for an uphill start in first gear
•	Observation	Normal observations
•	Manoeuvre	Prepare and release the handbrake (if not already done so)
		Slowly clutch up until the car moves
		Feet still
•	Exercise	Move slowly forwards using clutch control
		Steer to the right
		Over the crown, clutch down
		Steer to the left
		Move slowly forwards
		Check mirrors and signal if necessary
		Gently brake to a stop close to the kerb
		Apply handbrake. Make the car safe.

SKILLS DEVELOPMENT

The objective is to turn the car around to face the opposite direction using forward and reverse gears, without letting the tyres touch either kerb or entering a driveway.

Being able to demonstrate a turn in the road shows all the necessary skills to fully control a car.

This manoeuvre is colloquially known as the 'three point turn'. We avoid this term because it can be completed in more turns where necessary. Three points are a minimum, not a maximum!

Success with this manoeuvre requires the demonstration of three essential skills:

1. Vehicle control: coordinating the foot control and steering.

2. Accuracy: Steering briskly in the correct direction at the appropriate points.

3. Observation: being aware of any traffic, including pedestrians.

Eco-safe tip: Always perform your manoeuvres with a warm engine; it's much more eco-friendly!

Instruction Method: Use a diagram to explain each exercise and offer a demonstration. Below are some examples of questions that you might ask your learner. With experience you can devise your own bank of possible questions. Questions used must be appropriate to the learner and the circumstances of the lesson. Judge the balance of 'telling' and 'Q&A' on how the learner responds to your guidance.

Topic Key Point:	Sample Question:
Site	When and where may you turn the car in the road?
Width of road	How many turns will it take to turn the car round in this road?
Camber	How will you need to control the car when dealing with any camber in the road?
Aspects of the exercise	Can you remember the main aspects of the reversing exercises?

Illustration	Have you seen this diagram before?
POM	What routine will you use to begin each stage?
Accuracy	How quickly and in what manner will you need to turn the steering wheel?
Observation	Where will you need to look when:
	1. going forwards?
	2. reversing?
Finishing the exercise	How and where will you complete the exercise?

Typical faults to anticipate

Similar faults to reversing round a corner especially:

- Control – too fast (or too slow).
- Poor coordination of the controls including the handbrake.
- Accuracy – not completing in three points in a sufficiently wide road.
- Insufficient and/or 'shuffle' steering.
- Poor assessment of proximity of the kerb, particularly to rear when reversing.
- Observation – not looking in the correct directions.
- Indecision regarding waiting traffic.
- Not showing proper recognition of other road users.

Finally, as with all driving practise under instruction, complete the instructional core competencies by being sure that your learner knows and understands the causes of any driving faults and the solutions that you have provided.

LESSON XXI: TOWN DRIVING

KEY LEARNING POINTS

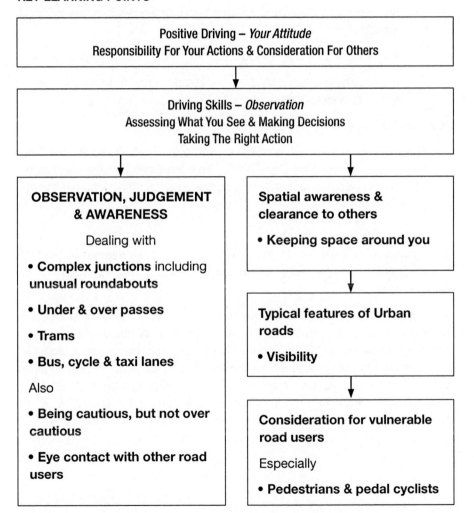

Positive Driving – *Your Attitude*
Responsibility For Your Actions & Consideration For Others

Driving Skills – *Observation*
Assessing What You See & Making Decisions
Taking The Right Action

**OBSERVATION, JUDGEMENT
& AWARENESS**

Dealing with

• **Complex junctions** including **unusual roundabouts**

• **Under & over passes**

• **Trams**

• **Bus, cycle & taxi lanes**

Also

• **Being cautious, but not over cautious**

• **Eye contact with other road users**

Spatial awareness & clearance to others

• **Keeping space around you**

Typical features of Urban roads

• **Visibility**

Consideration for vulnerable road users

Especially

• **Pedestrians & pedal cyclists**

Introduction

To become a 'Pass Plus' Instructor you will need to register with the DSA. This involves payment of a registration fee. In return you will be sent the resources you need to conduct the course. Before delivering a course:

- Review your DSA Instructor Guide.

- Prepare how you will explain DSA 'Pass Plus Pupil's Guide'.

- Confirm that during the course you will:

  - Complete the Training Report form / Progress Record

  - Sign and date each module, when your driver reaches the required standard

    A = Achieved E = Exceeded

    To pass the course, a satisfactory standard needs to be achieved in all the course modules.

At the end of the course

- The Training Record will need to be sent to the DSA. DSA will post the new driver a 'Pass Plus Certificate'. The intention is that the certificate number is used to claim any car insurance policy discounts that might be available.

Town Driving is one of the six practical in-car modules designed by the DSA to "accelerate the acquisition of driving experience and this improve the safety of new drivers".

Although the content of this module will have been covered pre-test, this is an opportunity to consolidate previous learning. We also know as ADIs, there's also always something new to learn. Our approach can be adapted, for instance, including focus on the **New Drivers Act**, such as how to avoid getting licence points and having to take another driving test. Also, by identifying the **main factors involved in collisions** experienced by young drivers.

STAGE OF ABILITY

- Newly Qualified Driver

RECAP

- Pre-test training and Driving Test
- Review/Introduction to 'Pass Plus'

Are there any known 'Town Driving' skills issues that still present risk of collision or incident?

CORE OF THE LESSON

What needs to be reviewed and prioritised?

- Eyesight and driving licence checks (if necessary).
- Familiarity with vehicle controls (might be customer's vehicle).
- Commitment to 'Pass Plus' – Attitude and accepting responsibility.
- Defensive driving – Reducing blameworthy risk on the road.
- Positive driving – Driver performance, not vehicle performance.

SKILLS DEVELOPMENT

The 'Pass Plus' town driving topics include:

- Observation, judgement and awareness.
- Anticipation of bus, lorry and motorcyclists.
- The importance of eye-contact.
- Dealing with vulnerable road users – pedestrians, especially children and pedal cyclists.
- Balancing making progress with being cautious.
- Good driving habits – Consider using the 'Smith System'.
- The consequences of getting it wrong.

Observation, judgement and awareness

Observation is the main component of anticipation.

Anticipation is the ability to identify, particularly developing hazards at the earliest opportunity. There are three main types of hazard:

1. **Physical features** such as road junctions, corners, bends and pedestrian crossings.

2. **The movement of other road users** such as other drivers, pedestrians and cyclists.

3. The **weather conditions** and how these can affect visibility and grip on the road surface.

Typical physical features of urban roads include:

*   multi-lane junctions
*   unusual roundabouts
*   bus and cycle lanes
*   under and over passes.

Urban roads – Physical hazards

Urban roads have many different types of permanent features, including the ones listed in this 'Pass Plus' module (above).

When a driver approaches these fixed hazards, there's often a traffic sign that warns or informs of what the hazard is. Signs that give orders can also determine who has the priority.

Topic details include **developing hazards** such as:

*   buses pulling out
*   lorries and the road space they need

- vehicles emerging

- riders coming up on the left

Reading the road – Developing hazards

Things do not just happen randomly, situations normally develop. As with the DSA's hazard perception test, all road users are "developing hazards". The anticipated movement of other drivers (eg buses, lorries and riders) is an important experience element for this module.

Training Route Planning:

- to ensure that your new driver has the maximum opportunity to learn and apply these skills.

COACHING DRIVER DEVELOPMENT

Using the 'Question and Answer' technique , along with prompts or commands where required develop the student's good driving habits using the 'Smith System':

1. **Looking well ahead** and planning.

2. **Move your eyes** – make eye contact, also check what's following behind and to the sides.

3. **Keeping space** around the vehicle – safe following distances.

4. **Spot the problems** – take up the correct road position and adjust speed, in plenty of time.

5. **Be seen** – when to use the headlights or signal, including using the horn.

Below are a few suggestions for coaching exercises. These can be adapted to suit your own preferences and your new driver's needs:

Coaching Exercise 1

Ask student to "look well ahead" and identify each traffic sign or road marking, prioritising if necessary, then:

1. comment how the information will affect their driving

2. "move the eyes" and say what is following behind

3. Say what they are going to do next, if anything (remaining three good driving habits)

Coaching Exercise 2

Ask student to suggest urban information/observation and action links. For instance:

Observation	**Look out for:**
Line of parked cars	Doors opening; vehicles moving off; pedestrians, including children stepping out

There are many other examples. How should drivers respond when they see:

1. an ice cream van?

2. a pedestrian hailing a taxi cab?

3. a traffic sign warning of school?

Coaching Exercise 3

Ask student to choose a hazard:

1. Ask – What can you see?

2. Ask – What can't be seen?

3. Ask – What can reasonably be expected to happen?

LESSON XXII: ALL WEATHER DRIVING

KEY LEARNING POINTS

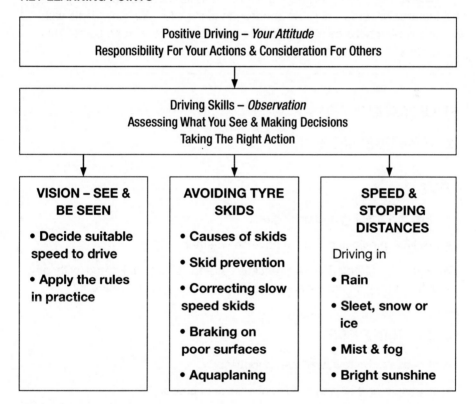

Positive Driving – *Your Attitude*
Responsibility For Your Actions & Consideration For Others

Driving Skills – *Observation*
Assessing What You See & Making Decisions
Taking The Right Action

**VISION – SEE &
BE SEEN**

• **Decide suitable
speed to drive**

• **Apply the rules
in practice**

**AVOIDING TYRE
SKIDS**

• **Causes of skids**

• **Skid prevention**

• **Correcting slow
speed skids**

• **Braking on
poor surfaces**

• **Aquaplaning**

**SPEED &
STOPPING
DISTANCES**

Driving in

• **Rain**

• **Sleet, snow or
ice**

• **Mist & fog**

• **Bright sunshine**

All Weather Driving is one of the six practical in-car modules designed by the DSA to "accelerate the acquisition of driving experience and improve the safety of new drivers".

Bad weather is often blamed for causing collisions when the actual cause is bad driving and inexperience. The weather can affect how far we can see and

how2become

how well our vehicle will perform. Whatever the weather always, "drive at a speed that will allow you to stop well within the distance you can see to be clear". ('Highway Code': Rule 126).

The aim of this module is to cover driving in adverse weather conditions. Some of the work in this module may have been covered pre-test.

Weather conditions – a type of hazard

When dealing with the first 'Pass Plus' module we covered the physical features/hazards such as bends, junctions etc. We also dealt with developing hazards that is, the movement of all other road users. This module covers the third type of hazard ...weather conditions.

STAGE OF ABILITY

- Newly Qualified Driver

RECAP

- Pre-test training and driving test
- Review previous driving in adverse weather

While this is intended as a practical session, to be integrated with other modules, it may be necessary to cover some of the topics in theory.

CORE OF THE LESSON

What needs to be reviewed and prioritised?

- Eyesight and driving licence checks (if necessary).
- Familiarity with vehicle controls (location of lights, wipers, washers and demisters).
- Vehicle and equipment (servicing, tyres and brakes).
- Different weather (any practical experience).
- Weather warnings (not to drive).

SKILLS DEVELOPMENT

The 'Pass Plus' all weather driving topics include:

1. Observation – vision
2. Assessing – Deciding – Acting
3. Skidding

1. **Observation – vision**. See and be seen. The effects on vision and correct use of the headlights in:

- rain
- sleet and snow
- mist and fog
- bright sunshine

Also:

- The importance of efficient windscreen wipers and washers
- Avoiding misting up by using the demisters
- Reflected and distracting light effects from wet roads at night; sun behind the landscape

Observation and vision

Use of headlights in bad weather

To improve road safety during daylight hours, new cars manufactured from February 2011 have to be fitted with daytime running lights (DRL). They don't have to be used, and it is possible to switch off DRL on some models of car. The advantage is that this lighting makes cars more visible to pedestrians crossing the road as well as other motorists.

- To be seen, dipped headlights on older cars should be used, whenever the windscreen wipers are needed. 'Highway Code', Rule 115 encourages use in dull daytime weather.

- In fog or falling snow at night, fog-lights will usually give a better view than dipped headlights. Fog-lights need only be used where visibility is down to 100 metres or less. These must be switched off when leaving the fog so as not to dazzle other drivers

- Rear fog-lights can mask brake lights, so, a larger separation distance is needed

---

Windscreen washers, wipers and demister

In low visibility be sure to:

- Make full use of the windscreen washers and wipers to keep the front windscreen as clear as possible. It's also important to keep the rear window clear as well.

- Top up the washer bottle with freeze resistant screen wash.

Bright sun

- Especially low in the sky on east/west sections of road can dazzle – use the visor.

- Can dazzle other drivers causing them to make mistakes.

---

2. **Assessing – Deciding – Acting** – The need to:

- Select the right speed in adverse weather conditions

- Maintain safe separation distances

Also:

- The Fog Code – advice in the 'Highway Code'

- Compensating for cross winds

- Road surfaces (grip and the effects of spray)

Perception of speed

Low visibility distorts our perception of speed:

- Check the speedometer regularly for the actual speed as our eyes may not accurately judge speed in these conditions.

Observing in low visibility

Keep a steady pace.

- Focus on what you can see, such as any vehicle in front, but avoid staring at the tail lights as this will draw you in too close. Also glance at the edge of the carriageway and the road ahead and be ready for the vehicle in front to stop suddenly.

At junctions:

- Wind your window down and listen for other traffic.
- Consider using the horn.

Crosswinds

- Where the carriageway is raised, such as in the countryside, be prepared for the effects of high winds. For instance, on viaducts and bridges.

3. **Skidding – the causes of skidding**

- Reactions of driver.
- Limitations of vehicle.
- Road conditions.

Also:

- Avoiding skids and correcting slow speed skids.
- The importance of good tyres and correct tyre pressures (as per manufacturer's handbook advice).
- Using a high gear and slow speed on poor surfaces.
- The vehicle's footprint.
- Braking distance on poor surfaces.

Skidding and the Road surface

Skidding

Preventing a skid is better than correcting one. If the vehicle is skidding the driver has got it wrong. Drivers must not rely on ABS and electronic stability programmes to keep themselves out of trouble.

- Most road surfaces are good for grip when they are clean and dry. Snow, ice, frost, rail, oil, muddy patches, wet leaves, dry loose dust or gravel can cause tyres to lose grip making a skid much more likely. Rain can produce a slippery road surface, especially after a long dry spell.

- In winter, there can be isolated or complete patches of ice or frost on some road surfaces. Sometimes they can be detected by their appearance or the behaviour of other road users. Tyres travelling on ice make virtually no noise.

- Be ready to adjust your driving very early to avoid getting into any kind of skid.

The 'Pass Plus' scheme deliberately excludes teaching high speed skidding. The worry is that this can encourage new drivers to attempt to practise this and increase the risk of a collision.

COACHING DRIVER DEVELOPMENT

Whatever the season or the weather, the topic areas can be coached using the 'Question and Answer' technique , along with any necessary prompts or commands.

Below are a few suggestions for coaching discussion areas. Some of the learning points overlap, so these points will need to be adapted to suit your own preferences and your new drivers' needs:

Coaching Exercises – Question/Discussion areas

1. Prior to the all weather driving session, ask your student to check the weather forecast for the date that the module will take place. Ask your student to prepare a driving weather plan. This should include details of any necessary pre-driving preparations.

2. At the beginning of the session ask your student to consider how the day's weather will affect any of the information/observation and action links for the types of road to be used.

3. Check your student's knowledge regarding how visibility and grip on the road surface is likely to be effected by the weather.

4. In good weather conditions check your student's knowledge of how driving is effected by:

   a) Bright sunshine

   b) Fog/mist

   c) Light/heavy rain – damp/wet conditions

   d) Wind

   e) Snow, ice and/or frost

   f) Possible combinations of any of the above

5. Check your student's knowledge of how the weather conditions described in Exercise 4 affect other types of road user.

6. Review what the stopping distances are in the wet and on ice; the types of skid and how these are caused.

7. Review the visibility of road markings and traffic signs/signals in types of poor weather conditions.

8. Review the use of headlights in poor weather conditions.

9. Briefly review the relevant safety features that are relevant to the weather conditions:

   a) ABS (Anti-lock brakes)

   b) ESP (Electronic Stability Programme)

c) Relevant safety checks, including the tyre tread depth and pressures

Also cover the benefits and/or disadvantages of driving front/rear wheel drive and 4x4 type vehicles.

10. Check your student's knowledge of what a micro-climate is and how this will affect their driving.

LESSON XXIII: OUT OF TOWN DRIVING AND RURAL ROADS

KEY LEARNING POINTS

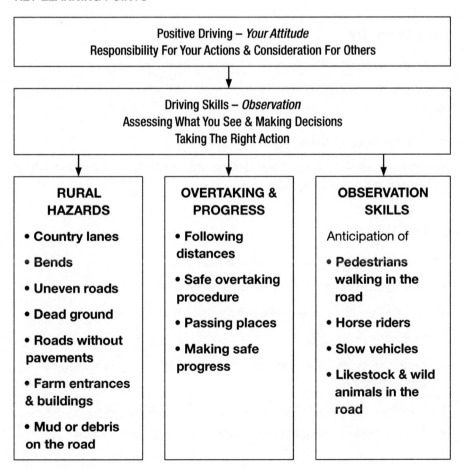

Positive Driving – *Your Attitude*
Responsibility For Your Actions & Consideration For Others

Driving Skills – *Observation*
Assessing What You See & Making Decisions
Taking The Right Action

RURAL HAZARDS

- Country lanes
- Bends
- Uneven roads
- Dead ground
- Roads without pavements
- Farm entrances & buildings
- Mud or debris on the road

OVERTAKING & PROGRESS

- Following distances
- Safe overtaking procedure
- Passing places
- Making safe progress

OBSERVATION SKILLS

Anticipation of

- Pedestrians walking in the road
- Horse riders
- Slow vehicles
- Likestock & wild animals in the road

Out of Town Driving and Rural Roads is one of the six practical in-car modules designed by the DSA to "accelerate the acquisition of driving experience and improve the safety of new drivers".

The aim of this module is to cover driving on roads away from town centres. These may well be semi-rural roads or could be narrow country lanes, depending on the roads that can be reached from your local area. If the opportunity is available, the practical session should include overtaking on single carriageway roads, timing the distance of any approaching traffic

Although the content of this module will have been covered pre-test, this is an opportunity to consolidate previous learning. There's also always something new to learn.

STAGE OF ABILITY

- Newly Qualified Driver

RECAP

Pre-test training and driving test.

Are there any known 'Out of Town Driving and Rural Road' skills issues that still present risk of collision or incident?

CORE OF THE LESSON

What needs to be reviewed and prioritised?

- Eyesight & driving licence checks (if necessary)
- Familiarity with vehicle controls (might be customer's vehicle)
- Visibility – limit points
- Defensive driving – anticipation, use of speed, making safe progress and overtaking
- Commercial and passenger vehicles – different speed limits
- Positive driving – driver performance, not vehicle performance

SKILLS DEVELOPMENT

The 'Pass Plus' out of town driving and rural roads topics should include differences with town driving such as:

1. Possibility of higher speeds.

2. Sharper bends.

3. More hills.

4. Greater opportunity for overtaking

Country Lanes:

- Consideration for pedestrians (roads without footpaths; looking out for horse riders; when and how to pass).

- Dealing with sharp bends (effective use of the horn).

- Awareness of farm buildings (slow moving vehicles; animals or mud on the road).

Other topics to be covered include:

- Observing the road ahead, especially in the middle and far distance.

- Keeping a safe distance from the vehicle ahead.

- Making progress safely.

- Dealing with bends (adjusting speed and correct positioning).

- Observing 'dead ground' early enough to see vehicles disappearing from view.

- Safe overtaking (effective use of mirrors; judging speed and intentions of approaching and overtaken traffic).

- Hills (the effect on a vehicle's performance and correct gear selection).

Route Planning:

- To ensure that your new driver has the maximum opportunity to learn and apply these skills.

1. Possibility of driving at higher speeds

On roads, where for instance the national speed limit applies, speed choice depends on:

- the prevailing road and traffic conditions

- the driver's own limitations (ability)

- familiarity with the vehicle being driven

At higher speeds we have to process more information in less time, so, we need to be fit and be able to give the task our undivided attention.

Coaching Exercise 1

While stationary, ask student what things are likely to affect our own perception of speed?

Answers should include such aspects as:

- Detail of the road type, surface condition and width.

- Visibility – traffic we see ahead and to our sides.

- Noise from the engine and the road.

- Comfort of the ride.

- What our own idea of what the speed should be.

- Our height off the ground.

- Power of the vehicle.

- Judging speed correctly after driving on fast roads.

1(a). Speeds of other vehicles

Speed limit signs tell us what the limit of particular roads is; there are also different limits of other types of vehicle.

To correctly anticipate the actions of commercial and passenger vehicles we must take into consideration that they have lower speed limits than cars on National Speed Limit (NSL) roads.

For instance, a bus or coach is legally restricted to 50mph on a single carriageway road and a large lorry is restricted to 40mph. Although these limits are higher on NSL dual carriageways and motorways, modern LGVs and PCVs engines are governed to lower limits.

- Revisit the vehicle speed limits table in the 'Highway Code'

Coaching Exercise 2

While stationary, ask student:

a) The different speed limits for different vehicles, for instance, a car towing a caravan on a NSL single carriageway road

   Answer: 50mph

b) Which LGVs have engines that you can expect to be governed to drive at not more than 56mph?

   Answer: As a safety and economy feature, European legislation requires all LGVs have to be fitted with a speed limiter set at 90 kph (56mph).

Coaching Exercise 3 – A Short Case Study

You are safely following an articulated lorry on a NSL single carriageway that is travelling at 40mph. Traffic and solid white lines provide no opportunities to overtake, so you settle behind at 40mph.

Half a mile later, you see the speed limit for the road change to 50mph. Is it legal for the LGV to increase its speed to 50mph?

- If not, explain why not?
- Discuss what can be anticipated and the best practice for each possible scenario

Coaching Exercise 4 – A Short Case Study

Often, on the back of LGVs you see a sign that reads "If you can't see my mirrors I can't see you".

Discuss the value and importance of this statement.

2. Sharper bends – Using 'Limit Points'

We always need to drive at a speed that we will always stop safely within the distance we can see to be clear.

To help ensure that we do this when driving on country lanes, we can use the 'limit point' of our vision ahead. Also known as the 'vanishing point', it is the last and furthest point ahead, where the roadside edges converge. It is the point where the road surface 'disappears' around the corner.

As you approach each limit point, the view ahead can open up away from you, or it may get closer, in which case, speed must be reduced and if the bend is sharp, the horn should be considered.

Coaching Exercise 5

Question for student. You are driving along a country lane without footpaths. Who and what should we be looking out for?

Answer: Pedestrians and also for horse riders.

3. More hills

In the rural environment, hills often combine with bends and junctions. To stay in control of our vehicle on faster roads, we need to be sure that we get the approach correct:

- Position for best visibility.

- Speed to be able to stop in distance seen to be clear.

 how2become

- Gear for the hill.

- Acceleration safely through the hazard(s).

At higher speeds, larger separation distances are needed from other vehicles that are in front. Otherwise the view ahead is more restricted and there will be less time to stop if things go wrong. Where there's closely following traffic, pressure needs to be applied to the brakes a little earlier as a signal for slowing/stopping.

Coaching Exercise 6

Ask your student: What is "dead ground"?

Answer: An area where there is a dip in the road where an approaching vehicle could be hidden.

---

4. Greater opportunity for overtaking

When overtaking on NSL country roads we need to consider the three main types of hazard:

1. Physical features including traffic signs and road markings.

2. The movement of other road users, particularly oncoming traffic.

3. The weather conditions, especially regarding the road surface.

Correct judgment of the speed and distance of traffic in front and any approaching traffic is important when deciding the necessity and safety of the intended overtake.

Coaching Exercise 7

Question for student:
On rural roads we are likely to come across animals. When we do, we need to pass them with plenty of room to spare and also be ready to stop. What must we not do?

Answer: We must not scare animals by sounding our horn, revving the engine or accelerating rapidly once we've passed them.

Ask student: If a road is blocked by a herd of animals what will we need to do?

Answer: We will need to stop and switch off the engine until they have left the road.

Coaching Exercise 8

Question for student:
When you see a warning sign for 'accompanied horses or ponies' you can expect to see horse riders. Horse-drawn vehicles are still sometimes seen on the roads. What must we do before overtaking a horse rider or horse drawn vehicle?

Answer:

- We must always pass wide and slowly. Horse riders may ride in double file when escorting a young or inexperienced horse or rider.

- Look out for signals from horse riders and horse drivers, be ready to heed a request to slow down or stop.

- Take great care and treat all horses as a potential hazard; they can be unpredictable, despite the efforts of their rider/driver.

COACHING DRIVER DEVELOPMENT

The 'Smith System' can be used during this module:

1. **Looking well ahead** and planning.

2. **Move your eyes** – check the mirror(s).

3. **Keeping space** around the vehicle – safe following distances.

4. **Spot the problems** – take up the correct road position and adjust speed, in plenty of time.

5. **Be seen** – when to use the headlights or signal, including using the horn.

Coaching Exercise 9

Ask student to suggest rural information/observation and action links. For instance:

Observation	**Look out for:**
Farm buildings	slow moving vehicles, such as tractors; animals or mud on the road.

There are many other examples. How should drivers respond when they see:

1. Country bus stop, no one waiting?

2. Fresh mud on road before a bend?

3. Centre line changes to a long white line with short gaps?

Coaching Exercise 10

While on the move, as a practical exercise, ask student to choose a hazard and:

1. Ask – What can you see?

2. Ask – What can't be seen?

3. Ask – What can reasonably be expected to happen?

LESSON XXIV: NIGHT DRIVING

KEY LEARNING POINTS

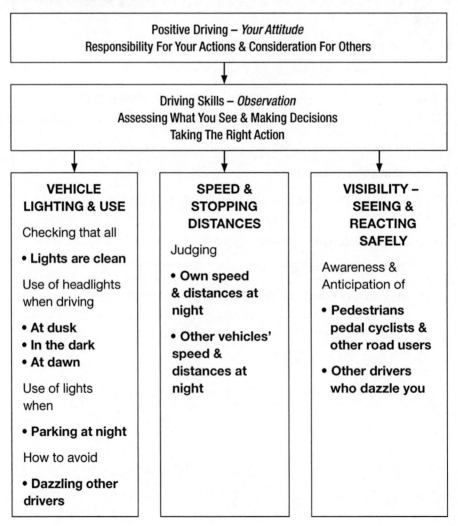

Positive Driving – *Your Attitude*
Responsibility For Your Actions & Consideration For Others

Driving Skills – *Observation*
Assessing What You See & Making Decisions
Taking The Right Action

VEHICLE LIGHTING & USE

Checking that all

- **Lights are clean**

Use of headlights when driving

- **At dusk**
- **In the dark**
- **At dawn**

Use of lights when

- **Parking at night**

How to avoid

- **Dazzling other drivers**

SPEED & STOPPING DISTANCES

Judging

- **Own speed & distances at night**
- **Other vehicles' speed & distances at night**

VISIBILITY – SEEING & REACTING SAFELY

Awareness & Anticipation of

- **Pedestrians pedal cyclists & other road users**
- **Other drivers who dazzle you**

Night Driving is one of the six practical in-car modules designed by the DSA to "accelerate the acquisition of driving experience and improve the safety of new drivers".

The aim of this module is to cover non-daylight driving conditions. This is a practical module that can be carried out on the same roads used for other modules. There are advantages in the new driver having to deal with the same roads in different conditions.

Even if this module has been covered pre-test, this is an opportunity to raise the issue that one of the main factors involved in serious traffic collisions is 'night driving'.

Fatal and serious traffic collisions happen mostly when driving at night and/or on weekends, particularly when carrying similarly aged passengers, and as a result of speeding.

- Alcohol and driving without seat belts remain key factors in young driver crashes and resulting deaths and injuries.

- Drug-driving, especially involving cannabis, is increasing, particularly among young men, and becomes especially dangerous when mixed with alcohol.

STAGE OF ABILITY

- Newly Qualified Driver

RECAP

- Pre-test training

Are there any known 'Night Driving' skills issues that still present risk of collision or incident?

CORE OF THE LESSON

What needs to be reviewed and prioritised?

- Eyesight & driving licence checks (if necessary).

- Familiarity with vehicle controls (location of headlight switches and clean windows inside as well as outside).

- Defensive driving – how this is effected where the field of vision is reduced.

- Positive driving – driver performance, not vehicle performance.

SKILLS DEVELOPMENT

The 'Pass Plus' Night Driving topics to include:

1. The importance of headlights.

2. Allowing time to adjust to the dark.

3. Driving at a speed so that you can stop within the distance you can see.

4. Driving at dusk and dawn.

5. Correct use of parking lights; main beam; dipped beam; driving lights and fog lights.

6. Dazzle.

7. Looking for pedestrians.

8. Being prepared for cyclists.

9. Differences between lit town roads and unlit open roads, compensating for the transition.

Route Planning:

- To ensure that your new driver has the maximum opportunity to learn and apply these skills.

- Possible use of the same routes as for other modules.

1. The importance of headlights

Checks that the lights:

- are clean
- operating properly
- are correctly adjusted

Coaching Exercise 1

While stationary, ask student to check the headlight settings.

---

2. Allowing time to adjust to the dark

It will help by:

- cleaning windscreens, windows and all mirrors

Coaching Exercise 2

While stationary confirm with student that the vehicle's glass is clean

Coaching Exercise 3

While stationary ask student what the effects of the daylight dwindling are:

Answers can include:

- difficulty seeing information
- contrast falls
- colours fade
- edges become indistinct
- extra strain on the eyes

3. Driving at a speed so that you can stop within the distance you can see

This means, never driving so fast that you can't stop within the range of the headlights.

Coaching Exercise 4

Ask your student for the reasons why this is correct.

Answer:

- Vision is more limited at night meaning that less information is available. It follows that drivers can't drive as fast at night as may be safe in the daylight.

Confirm that if it's not possible to stop safely within the range of the headlights then the car is travelling too fast.

---

4. Driving at dusk and dawn

Adapting our driving for sunset and sunrise means that we need to know how to:

- Compensate for half-light conditions

We also need to take into account changing weather conditions, including rain. Some wet road surfaces can reflect light and affect what you can or cannot see ahead.

Coaching Exercise 5

Ask your student how it is possible to compensate for half light conditions.

Answer:

- Allow time for eyes to adjust. If this is difficult, recommend a professional eyesight check.
- Be ready to use the headlights earlier at dusk, especially when driving a dark coloured car.
- At dawn, leave the headlights on longer.
- Confirm answers to Exercise Three, if necessary.

how2become

5. The correct use of lights

The correct use of lights is controlled by legislation and is documented in the 'Highway Code'. Questions are also included in the Theory section of the driving test.

Coaching Exercise 6

Check your student's previous knowledge by asking, when it will be necessary to use:

a) Parking lights.

b) Main beam.

c) Dipped beam.

d) Driving lights.

e) Fog lights.

Example answers:

a) Parking lights must be used, for instance, where the speed limit for the road exceeds 30mph.

b) Main beam will increase the range of vision, typically outside towns, on unlit country roads.

c) Dipped beam must be used outside built up areas.

d) Driving lights, whether dipped, or main beam should be used to suit the prevailing road and traffic conditions.

e) Fog lights must only be used where visibility is seriously reduced, that is to less than 200 metres (328 feet).

6. Dazzle

Headlights of vehicles shining directly into drivers' eyes will cause dazzle.

Coaching Exercise 7

Check your student's previous knowledge by asking:

a) How can they avoid dazzling other drivers?

b) What should they do if they are dazzled by other drivers?

Example answers:

a) Switch from full beam to dipped beam where other drivers are likely to be dazzled, for instance, where there is approaching traffic, or before overtaking.

b) Slow down, look towards the nearside kerb.

7. Looking for pedestrians

Although there will be street lights in built-up areas, the lighting can cause patches of shadow that may hide vulnerable road users, such as pedestrians, including joggers that are not wearing bright or fluorescent clothing.

Coaching Exercise 8

Ask student to make an intelligent prediction where pedestrians may step out into the road at night.

Example answer

Observation	Look out for:
Pub at closing time	Tired, possibly intoxicated pedestrians.

8. Being prepared for cyclists

Cycling is being encouraged as an eco-friendly and more healthy means of transport, so we need to be asking ourselves when and where we can expect to see cyclists.

Coaching Exercise 9

Ask student how they will look out for cyclists.

Example answer

Look for areas of shadows caused by street lighting that may conceal cyclists wearing dark clothes.

Confirm this with student and add:

Many cyclists will follow the advice in the 'Highway Code', including about wearing light coloured or fluorescent clothing. Some cyclists do not follow all the rules and may even cross red lights and ride on the pavement, so we have to always expect the 'unexpected'.

9. Differences between lit town roads and unlit open roads and how to compensate for the transition

Built-up areas in some towns can be quite bright. Going from these roads to unlit ones can affect your eyes.

Coaching Exercise 9

Ask student for any local examples of where this might happen.

Coaching Exercise 10

Ask student what the differences are and how they should respond.

Example answer

When driving from a well it area into one that is unlit, the eyes will need some time to adjust to the lower level of lighting. Where there is traffic

on unlit roads this can help to provide information, such as the sweep of the headlights of vehicles ahead approaching a bend can give some indication as to how sharp the bend is, also the brake lights of vehicles in front can provide an early warning to reduce speed.

Confirm this with student and add:

On unlit roads we need to reply on 'cats-eyes' more and take notice of the black and white 'hazard marker posts' with red/white reflectors.

LESSON XXV: DUAL CARRIAGEWAYS

KEY LEARNING POINTS

Positive Driving – *Your Attitude*
Responsibility For Your Actions & Consideration For Others

Driving Skills – *Observation*
Assessing What You See & Making Decisions
Taking The Right Action

JOINING & LEAVING

- Traffic signs: Primary & non-primary routes

- Joining: effective observation

- Leaving: return to two-way roads & possible change of speed limit

- Use of slip roads

FORWARD PLANNING & OBSERVATION

- Effective observation including use of mirrors & blindspots

- Scanning near, middle & far distance

- Acting on traffic signs, signals & road markings

- Appropriate use of speed in different circumstances

- Following distances including the two second rule

- Courtesy to other road users

- Use of lights, including headlights & hazard lights

OVERTAKING

- Keeping distance/ space

- Lane discipline

Dual Carriageways is one of the six practical in-car modules designed by the DSA to "accelerate the acquisition of driving experience and improve the safety of new drivers".

Even if this module has been covered pre-test, this is a practical opportunity to prepare for motorway driving. Dual carriageways often combine traffic moving at the same high speeds as on motorways with additional hazards such as junctions and slower moving vehicles and the absence of a hard shoulder.

The aim of this module is to cover defensive driving on two or three-lane high speed dual carriageways. As with any of the modules covered earlier, all the driving skills required can be efficiently delivered using the 'Smith System'.

STAGE OF ABILITY

- Newly Qualified Driver

RECAP

- Pre-test training and driving test

Are there any known 'Dual Carriageway' skills issues that still present risk of collision or incident?

CORE OF THE LESSON

What needs to be reviewed and prioritised?

- Eyesight & driving licence checks (if necessary).

- Familiarity with vehicle controls (might be customer's vehicle).

- Defensive driving – reducing blameworthy risk on the road.

- Positive driving – driver performance, not vehicle performance.

SKILLS DEVELOPMENT

The 'Pass Plus' Dual Carriageway topics include:

1. Effective observation.

2. Judgement and planning.

3. Turning left from and onto dual carriageways.

4. Turning right from dual carriageways.

5. Turning right onto dual carriageways.

Route Planning to:

- Ensure that your new driver has the maximum opportunity to learn and apply these skills.

- Manage the time effectively and pre-determine any periods of independent driving.

---

1. Effective observation

This includes:

- Early and frequent use of the mirrors.

- Dealing with blind spots.

- Continual re-assessment of the movement of other road users, especially those ahead, alongside and behind.

- Scanning the near, middle and far distance, and changing focus between them.

Coaching Exercise – Using the 'Smith System'

For example, on the move, ask student what they see when:

- Looking well ahead (visually scanning the near, middle and far distance).

- Moving the eyes (checking all mirrors, ensuring that any vehicles in the blind areas are identified).

On the move:

- Keeping space (is there a safety cushion ahead and to the sides of the vehicle?).

On the move:

- What possible problems can be seen (junctions including roundabouts, service buses pulling out of bus lay-bys, changing traffic patterns)?

- Be seen (use of headlights, signals or road positioning).

2. Judgement and planning

When:

- Joining from slip roads.

- Adjusting speed to fit in with the movement of other traffic.

- Keeping a safe distance from the vehicle ahead (the two second rule).

- Overtaking: deciding when it is safe, allowing enough time, using the MSM routine, moving back to the left without cutting in.

- Anticipating when the road becomes single carriageway: looking for signs, observing the far distance, reducing speed.

Introduce this section as:

1. Joining the dual carriageway (Use of the Mirror(s), Signal Manoeuvre routine).

2. Driving along the dual carriageway (Use of Speed, Positioning and Lane discipline, Overtaking).

3. Leaving the dual carriageway (Use of the Mirror(s), Signal Manoeuvre routine).

Coaching Exercise 2 – Using the 'Smith System'

Interact with the student on the move using the 'Smith System'. For example:

- Look well ahead (what can be seen, what can't be seen, what can we reasonably expect to happen?).

- Move the eyes (checking mirrors, comparing view in interior mirror with both exterior mirrors).

- Keep space (from vehicles in front and avoid being three abreast).

- Spot the problems (fixed features such as junctions, moving features such as traffic and environmental features such as the condition of the road surface).

- Be seen (on faster roads, the use of headlights and signals in plenty of time).

---

3. Turning left from and onto dual carriageways

What type of join or exit?

- Traditional junction (standard emerge/exit)
- Slip road (acceleration/deceleration lane)

Coaching Exercise 3

Ask student how the different type of junction affects:

1. Approach position and speed.

2. Judging the traffic speed and looking for safe gaps to emerge/exit.

---

4. Turning right from dual carriageways

What information can be seen?

- Primary/Non-primary route traffic signs giving route directions.
- Traffic signs and/or road markings giving lane advice.
- Uncontrolled or controlled by traffic light signals.

What types of junction layout can be expected?

- Traditional junction

- Slip/filter lane

Coaching Exercise 4 – Use 'Smith System', for instance:

On the move, ask student to look well ahead and identify all or any of the above.

---

5. **Turning right onto dual carriageways**

What information can be seen?

- Primary/Non-primary route traffic signs giving route directions.

- Traffic signs and/or road markings giving lane advice.

- Uncontrolled or controlled by traffic light signals.

Where the junction is uncontrolled, crossing the first carriageway before turning right will call for excellent observation skills.

Coaching Exercise 5

Ask student:

- To assess the width of the central reservation (Is there enough room to protect the full length of the vehicle? (What do we do if there isn't enough room?).

- How to judge the speed and distance of approaching traffic and at which point it will be safe to emerge.

---

6. **High speed navigation on dual carriageways**

Coaching Exercise 6

Dual carriageways on A-class roads will often carry a considerable volume of traffic at high speeds. These roads are not built to the same standard of motorways, but do require the same observation skills and techniques.

As a final practical coaching exercise, determine a pre-set route that involves the student independently following primary route signs and information at speeds above 40mph and where possible the national speed limit.

The focus of this exercise should include use of primary and non-primary route traffic signs as well attention to all relevant road markings. If you haven't already done so elsewhere, introduce how satellite navigation equipment should be correctly used.

Before taking the motorway training and development, complete this module by making a professional review and summary of all progress made.

LESSON XXVI: MOTORWAY DRIVING

KEY LEARNING POINTS

Positive Driving – *Your Attitude*
Responsibility For Your Actions & Consideration For Others

↓

Driving Skills – *Observation*
Assessing What You See & Making Decisions
Taking The Right Action

↓

Planning Journeys
Route Planning / Vehicle Condition / Sufficient Fuel & Other Vehicle Checks

↓

JOINING & LEAVING

- Traffic signs, signals & road markings

- Joining: effective observation

- Leaving procedure: return primary / non-primary routes / dual carriageway or two-way roads & possible change of speed limit

- Use of slip roads

FORWARD PLANNING & OBSERVATION

- Effective observation including use of mirrors & blind spots

- Scanning near, middle & far distance

- Acting on traffic signs, signals & road markings

- Appropriate use of speed in different circumstances

- Following distances including the 'two second rule'

- Courtesy to other road users

- Use of lights, including headlights & hazard lights

OVERTAKING

- Keeping distance/ space

- Lane discipline

Motorway Driving is one of the six practical in-car modules designed by the DSA to "accelerate the acquisition of driving experience and improve the safety of new drivers".

This module should only be covered in theory where there is no motorway nearby. If this is the case, the student must follow up with practical experience as soon as possible afterwards.

The aim of this module is to give the new driver confidence and relate defensive driving techniques to motorway driving. As with any of the modules covered earlier, all the driving skills required can be efficiently delivered using the 'Smith System'.

STAGE OF ABILITY

- Newly Qualified Driver

RECAP & REVIEW

- The driving skills needed for successful 'Motorway Driving'.
- The meaning of "positive driving" for all six modules.

CORE OF THE LESSON

What needs to be reviewed and prioritised?

- Eyesight & driving licence checks (if necessary).
- Familiarity with vehicle controls (might be customer's vehicle).
- Defensive driving – reducing blameworthy risk on the road.
- Positive driving – driver performance, not vehicle performance.

SKILLS DEVELOPMENT

The 'Pass Plus' Motorway topics include:

1. Absence of a number of hazards.
2. Positive driving skills.

3. Speed and collisions.

4. Review of driving skills, especially dual carriageways.

Route Planning to:

- Ensure that your new driver has the maximum opportunity to learn and apply these skills.

- Manage the time effectively and pre-determine any periods of independent driving.

---

1. Absence of a number of hazards

Motorways are the safest roads because of the absence of:

- pedestrians and cyclists

- oncoming traffic and vehicles turning right

- roundabouts

Coaching Exercise 1

Ask student:

- What makes motorway roads different from all other roads?

Confirm that the absence of pedestrians, cyclists, oncoming and right turning traffic results in fewer collisions, making this kind of road the safest type.

While there are some close similarities with driving on high speed dual carriageways, some differences will need introduction. Ask your student what these are. Answers include:

- Slip roads for joining and leaving the motorway, that are not always present on multi-lane dual carriageways.

- The limited opportunities for refuelling and refreshments.

- The dangers of stopping on the hard shoulder in an emergency.

- The legal restrictions on vehicles permitted to use the motorway.

2. Positive Driving Skills

Defensive driving:

- effective observation and

- good anticipation

Introduce this section as:

1. Joining the motorway (Use of the Mirror(s), Signal Manoeuvre routine).

2. Driving along the motorway (Use of Speed, Positioning and Lane discipline, Overtaking).

3. Leaving the motorway (Use of the Mirror(s), Signal Manoeuvre routine).

Coaching Exercise 2 – Risk Assessment

Ask your student to list all the possible risks affecting the driver's ability to concentrate at motorway speeds in varying levels of traffic density. Answers can include:

- Monotonous driving conditions.

- Feelings such as tiredness, stress or mood.

Consider with your student how these issues might be overcome, such as journey planning and taking enough breaks.

Ask your student:

- What vehicle checks need to be made before driving on a motorway?

- What do you need to do if you have to pull up on the motorway's hard shoulder, because of a vehicle breakdown?

3. Speed and Collisions

Because of the high speeds involved, motorway collisions tend to be more serious. Developing accuracy in assessing road speeds and stopping distances under fast moving traffic conditions can take some time, depending on the student's own ability and confidence.

New drivers should:

- Drive within their own ability and competence.

- Steadily develop their experience to become comfortable and confident with increased speed ranges.

Coaching Exercise 3 – Preparing for speed:

High speed means that hazardous situations can develop quickly meaning that we travel further before we respond. Ask your student the best way to prepare for practise.

4. Review of driving skills, especially dual carriageways

Reinforce the appropriate skills covered in the previous modules, especially Module 5, including:

- Joining motorways from slip roads.

- Good anticipation – reading the road ahead.

- Continual re-assessment of the movement of other vehicles.

- Separation distances.

- Safe overtaking, including the different speed limits for articulated goods vehicles and cars towing caravans or trailers.

Coaching Exercise 4 – Using the Smith System

As in Module 5, interact with the student on the move using the 'Smith System'. For example:

- Look well ahead (what can be seen, what can't be seen, what can we reasonably expect to happen?).

- Move the eyes (checking mirrors, comparing view in interior mirror with both exterior mirrors).

- Keep space (from vehicles in front and avoid being three abreast).

- Spot the problems (fixed features such as junctions – joining and exiting, moving features such as different types of vehicle and environmental features such as the condition of the road surface).

- Be seen (on faster roads, the use of headlights and signals in plenty of time).

LESSON XXVII: ADVANCED DRIVING

KEY LEARNING POINTS

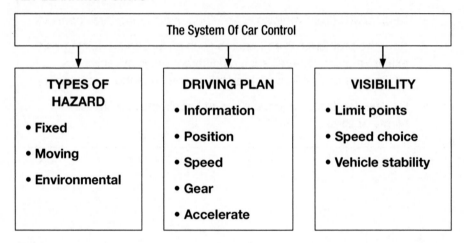

The System Of Car Control

TYPES OF HAZARD

- Fixed
- Moving
- Environmental

DRIVING PLAN

- Information
- Position
- Speed
- Gear
- Accelerate

VISIBILITY

- Limit points
- Speed choice
- Vehicle stability

STAGE OF ABILITY

- Fully Qualified Driver

RECAP

- Level of experience since passing the driving test.
- Any blameworthy collisions or incidents.
- Expectations and confidence.

CORE OF THE SESSION

What needs to be prioritised?

- Driving licence and eyesight check (if necessary).
- Familiarity with vehicle and pre-driving checks.
- The three types of road & traffic hazard.
- Limit points to visibility.
- The system of car control.

SKILLS DEVELOPMENT

Defensive driving techniques

- Anticipation – What CAN be seen? What CANNOT be seen? What might be REASONABLY expected to happen?
- The 'Smith System' (5 Good Driving Habits).
- Eco-Safe Driving.
- Commentary Driving.

VALIDATION

Performance evaluation

- Has the driver responded well to your coaching?
- Risk assessment – Low, Medium or High?
- How much further training is needed?

ACTION PLAN

What next?

- Agree areas for further practice and improvement.
- Determine any new objectives.

Coaching Exercise 1

The three types of hazard.

At appropriate times on the move, ask the driver to identify 'information' ahead, giving examples of:

- Fixed/physical features.

- Moving features (developing hazards).

- Environmental features (How road surface is affected by the weather).

With the fixed features, begin by asking the driver to identify any traffic signs or road markings, stating their correct meaning, along with how the information effects their driving.

Coaching Exercise 2

Chasing the Limit Point. On single carriageway, national speed limit roads, ask the driver to tell you when the limit point is:

- Getting closer. Is the driver slowing down?

- Becoming further away? Is the driver accelerating, if safe to do so.

- Is the driver able to stop safely, in the distance seen to be clear?

Coaching Exercise 3

The flexibility of the system of car control. Ask the driver to identify the features:

- Information – what is the next hazard?

- Position – where should the vehicle be positioned?

- Speed – brakes too slow, where needed.

- Gear – to go. Which one?

- Acceleration – smooth and progressive through the hazard.

Depending on driver's knowledge and experience, compare the system of car control with MSPSL.

Coaching Exercise 4

Defensive driving techniques. In both urban and rural environments, ask the driver:

- What CAN be seen ahead?

- What CANNOT be seen?

- What might be REASONABLY expected to happen?

Link this with Coaching Exercise 1.

Coaching Exercise 5

The 'Smith System'. Identify the five Good Driving Habits and link with the previous four coaching exercises. Ask and confirm these five points with the driver:

- Look well ahead – determine relevant information. What is the escape route or alternative plan, if things go wrong?

- Move your eyes – use the appropriate mirrors. How should you respond to what you see?

- Keep space – never too close to the vehicle in front, be able to stop in distance seen to be clear.

- Spot the problems – which hazard types do we need to prioritise in the circumstances?

- Be seen – do we need to signal? How? Using indicators, lights and/or the horn?

Coaching Exercise 6

EcoSafe driving techniques. Ask the driver to consider their driving style and confirm:

- Correct speed choice/avoiding needlessly high engine revs, harsh acceleration and braking.

- Smooth use of gas pedal, 'feathering' it lightly and evenly to adjust driving speed.

- Appropriate gear choice for economy driving.

- When safety factors override economy consideration.

- When to use cruise control.

- Manoeuvring on a warm engine.

- Use of vehicle with/without stop/start technology.

- When to open windows or use the air conditioning.

- Pre-driving checks eg tyre pressures and vehicle load.

Coaching Exercise 7

Commentary Driving:

1. Run through the pre-driving vehicle checks and identify local knowledge.

2. On the move, begin by identifying all traffic signs and road markings.

3. Next, link these with the three types of hazard.

4. Either, talk through driving plan (IPSGA – the system of car control).

    - What CAN be seen?

    - What CANNOT be seen?

    - What might be REASONABLY expected to happen?

5. Talk through the five Good Driving Habits

The driving style needs to be proactive and the commentary needs to reflect this.

LESSON XXVIII: CORPORATE DRIVER TRAINING

KEY LEARNING POINTS

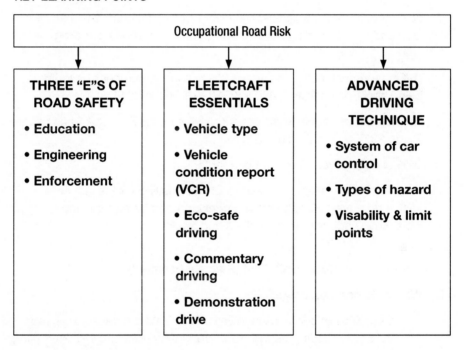

Occupational Road Risk

THREE "E"S OF ROAD SAFETY

- Education
- Engineering
- Enforcement

FLEETCRAFT ESSENTIALS

- Vehicle type
- Vehicle condition report (VCR)
- Eco-safe driving
- Commentary driving
- Demonstration drive

ADVANCED DRIVING TECHNIQUE

- System of car control
- Types of hazard
- Visability & limit points

STAGE OF ABILITY

- Fully Qualified Driver/Experienced Motorist

RECAP

- Level of driving experience.

- Any blameworthy collisions or incidents.

- Expectations and confidence.

CORE OF SESSION

- **Occupational Road Risk Brief (Important statistics).**

i. The average motorist drives about 8,000 miles a year.

ii. Fleet Drivers are exposed to more risk of collisions because of their higher mileage.

iii. 95% of collisions are caused by driver error and around one third of fatal and serious road crashes involve someone who was driving for work.

iv. The most recent statistics show a 3% rise in the number of people being killed, rising from 1,850 in 2010 to 1,901 in 2011.

v. The number of people killed or seriously injured (KSI) in 2011 has risen 2% to 25,023 from 24,510 in 2010.

vi. 46% of all fatalities were car occupants.

vii. Vehicle traffic levels are broadly stable after falling for the last three years and adverse weather is not considered to be factor in the increase in serious road casualties and fatalities.

- **Occupational Road Risk Brief (Risk assessment)**

i. **Where do crashes occur?**

  - Over 50% of collisions involve vehicles that are travelling ahead; 15% are rounding bends, 15% are turning right and 4% overtaking.

ii. **What are the financial and human costs of collisions?**

  - The average fatal collision costs society is £1,585,510 per death.

  - The total yearly cost of collisions is in the region of £15billion.

  - The human cost involves pain, grief and suffering to the casualty, relatives and friends, as well as the intrinsic loss of enjoyment of life in the case of fatalities.

iii. how does driver development bring about benefits to both employers and employees?

- Contributes towards safer driving for work and leisure, making driving more relaxing, reducing stress and risk of incident/collisions.

- Reduces business downtime, improving productivity, efficiency and improving company image.

- Savings on insurance, fuel, repairs and maintenance costs.

- **Occupational Road Risk Brief (Enforcement)**
Police investigating fatal road collisions treat these as "unlawful killings until the contrary is proved". They will determine whether anyone involved was at work, and if so, did this factor contribute towards the collision. Health & Safety offences can be aimed at Company Managers and Directors who have a duty of care for employees.

- **Eyesight and Driving Licence Check**

i. Eyesight check – to at least the minimum standard for a car licence.

ii. Check for appropriate category entitlement on driving licence, including counter-part paper section for validity. DVLA licence checks can now be made direct or through third party agencies at an agreed fee, either online or over the phone.

- **Vehicle Condition Report (VCR)/Vehicle Type**

i. The vehicle used must be fit for purpose, roadworthy and taxed. The level of pre-driving checks will depend on the vehicle type. For a car or van, the "POWER" (Petrol/Fuel – Oil – Water – Electrics – Rubber) routine is a minimum check. A VCR check will include:

> **Tyres** – pressure / tread depth and no defects.
>
> **Lights** – all working. No damage or defects.
>
> **Indicators** – all working. No damage or defects.
>
> **Vision** – Windows clean, legal and undamaged.

> **Fluid levels** – Oil, coolant, washers, power steering, brake fluid and clutch fluid.
>
> **Body condition** – internal and/or external damage.
>
> **Load safety** – no loose items in the cabin and heavy/outside items secured.

ii.   The driver's familiarity with the vehicle type needs to be confirmed, for instance, its performance and handling, control settings, use of navigation systems and other technologies.

SKILLS DEVELOPMENT / PRACTICAL FLEETCRAFT

The coaching session needs to be interactive. The essential areas of 'Roadcraft' that you need to cover are the same as for 'advanced driving':

i.   **THREE TYPES OF HAZARD** – Three categories. Fixed/physical features; Moving features (developing hazards) and Environmental features (Road surface/weather).

ii.   **SYSTEM OF CAR CONTROL** – "IPSGA" (Information – Position – Speed – Gear – Acceleration).

iii.   **LIMIT POINT** of vision ahead – Use on country lanes where speed limits are higher.

For each of these three areas, coaching for skill development and feedback should focus on the driver's:

a)   Acceleration and braking patterns.

b)   Corner and lane handling.

c)   Speed handing.

d)   Judgement of traffic movement (other road users) based on the above three points, points a) to c).

- **Coaching / Driver development format**

Briefly introduce your coaching plan including any recap of previous learning or assessment. Coaching and prompts should be delivered in a predominantly conversational manner.

i. **ASSESSMENT** – Judge the client's needs, the training / development route and your own preferences

ii. **POSITIVE FEEDBACK** – cover any habits and focus on best practice with immediate feedback. Use mostly Q&A method and prompts, coaching, along with direct instruction where needed.

iii. **ANTICIPATION** – What CAN be seen? What CANNOT be seen? What might be REASONABLY expected to happen? Also consider using the 'Smith System' (5 Good Driving Habits).

iv. **ECOSAFE DRIVING** – Reducing fuel costs; minimising wear and tear on the vehicle are amongst the benefits to be achieved from a defensive driving style.

v. **COMMENTARY DRIVING** – Consider ability. Begin with identifying traffic signs and road markings and how these affect the driving plan (system of car control). Link with the three main types of hazard and anticipation.

vi. **MANOEUVRE** – Consider one set-piece manoeuvre, that includes reversing, followed by a 'return development run' back to base.

vii. **DEMONSTRATION DRIVE** – A short low risk demonstration, if this will benefit the driver.

viii. **VALIDATION** – Before the end of the session, evaluate client's response to your coaching.

- **Risk Assessment**

At the end of the session

i. **ACHIEVEMENTS** – Summarise the learning points.

ii. **ACTION PLAN** – Driver to write down areas for further practise and improvement. Briefly discuss and agree objectives for next session or a summary of the 'Report to Company' where this is requested.

iii. **REPORT RISK PROFILE BACK TO COMPANY** – Low, Medium or High?

TEN FLEET COACHING EXERCISES

Depending on the individual needs of each driver, these can be the same as for advanced driving. We've included a couple more and you can of course include any of your own addition exercises.

Feel free to adapt the ten exercises listed below to suit your client's needs and/or local conditions.

Coaching Exercise 1

The three types of hazard.

At appropriate times on the move, ask the driver to identify information ahead, giving examples of:

- Fixed/physical features.

- Moving features (developing hazards).

- Environmental features (how road surface is affected by the weather).

With the fixed features, begin by asking the driver to identify any traffic signs or road markings, stating their correct meaning, along with how the information affects their driving.

Suggest to the driver that they devise INFORMATION and ACTION LINKS. For example, Bus Stop = Bus route; School Warning Sign = Check time of day, observe for children. How many other examples can the driver come up with?

Coaching Exercise 2

Chasing the Limit Point. On single carriageway, national speed limit roads, ask the driver to tell you when the limit point is:

- Getting closer. Is the driver slowing down?

- Becoming further away? Is the driver accelerating, if safe to do so.

- Is the driver able to stop safely, in the distance seen to be clear?

Coaching Exercise 3

The flexibility of the system of car control. Ask the driver to identify the features:

- Information – what is the next hazard?
- Position – where should the vehicle be positioned?
- Speed – brakes to slow, where needed.
- Gear – to go. Which one?
- Acceleration – smooth and progressive through the hazard.

Include mirror(s) use between each of the five features. Ask the driver what is following behind or to the side and how close or far away the vehicle(s) is/ are. Where appropriate, ask what is the benefit of monitoring following traffic?

Coaching Exercise 4

Defensive driving techniques/Anticipation. In both urban and rural environments, ask the driver:

- What CAN be seen ahead?
- What CANNOT be seen?
- What might be REASONABLY expected to happen?

Link this with Coaching Exercise 1.

Coaching Exercise 5

The 'Smith System'. Identify the five Good Driving Habits and link with the previous four coaching exercises. Ask and confirm these five points with the driver:

- Look well ahead – determine relevant information. What is the escape route or alternative plan, if things go wrong?
- Move your eyes – use the appropriate mirrors. How should you respond to what you see?
- Keep space – never too close to the vehicle in front, be able to stop in distance seen to be clear.
- Spot the problems – which hazard types do we need to prioritise in the circumstances?

- Be seen – do we need to signal? How? Indicators, lights and/or the horn?

Coaching Exercise 6

Do you coast?

Not in the sense of selecting neutral gear or depressing the clutch too early, but rather how you commit yourself to the driving task?

Devise a mnemonic that will help you to remember the key elements of fleetcraft using the word COAST or any other suitable words.

Suggested answer:

C oncentration
O bservation
A nticipation
S pace
T ime

Coaching Exercise 7

What are your 'Zones of Visibility' for instance approaching a roundabout or before overtaking?

How is correct road positioning important?

1. Are you positioned for the best visibility?

2. Can you fake it?

3. What is faking it?

4. How do you approach junctions, plan to stop and look to go?

Discuss examples of:

Better Driving Matrix

Position	Fake Space	Slow
for	to	until
Vision	**Make Space**	**Know**
for	to	then
Decision	**Take Space**	**Go**

Coaching Exercise 8

EcoSafe driving techniques. Ask the driver to consider their driving style and confirm:

- Correct speed choice / avoiding needlessly high engine revs, harsh acceleration and braking.

- Smooth use of gas pedal, 'feathering' it lightly and evenly to adjust driving speed.

- Appropriate gear choice for economy driving.

- When safety factors override economy consideration.

- When to use cruise control.

- Manoeuvring on a warm engine.

- Use of vehicle with/without stop/start technology.

- When to open windows or use the air conditioning.

- Pre-driving checks eg tyre pressures and vehicle load.

Coaching Exercise 9

Commentary Driving:

1. Run through the pre-driving vehicle checks and identify local knowledge.

2. On the move, begin by identifying all traffic signs and road markings.

3. Next, link these with the three types of hazard.

4. Talk through driving plan (IPSGA – The system of car control).

- What CAN be seen?

- What CANNOT be seen?

- What might be REASONABLY expected to happen?

5. Talk through the five Good Driving Habits

The driving style needs to be proactive and the commentary should reflect this.

Coaching Exercise 10

National speed limit for lorries and buses. Where the situation arises, check driver's knowledge of the speed limit for:

- A bus, coach, mini-bus or goods vehicle (not exceeding 7.5 tonnes maximum laden weight) driving on single/dual carriageway roads and motorways.

- A large goods vehicle, exceeding 7.5 tonnes maximum laden weight driving on single/dual carriageway roads and motorways.

- Cars towing caravans or trailers.

Discussion point: Through European legislation, the maximum speed that LGVs or PCVs can be driven is restricted by limiters fitted to the vehicle. How does this affect your anticipation of other road users?

APPENDIX 3
DSA DRIVING TEST REPORT FORM (DL25)

As a car, bus or lorry instructor, you need to be fully conversant with the Driving Test Report form, known as the "DL25". Copies of the form are available at Driving Test Centres and comprehensive guidance notes are incorporated in the document.

During your training, make yourself familiar with the routine for accompanying a learner driver, when attending a driving test. As you gain experience as an instructor, depending on the availability of driving test centres, you will develop your own preference of choice and advise your customers accordingly. You are encouraged to sit-in on driving tests or at least listen to the de-brief at the end. Doing this helps you to make sense of the DL25.

Driving Test Report

DL25A
0407

I declare that:

- the use of the test vehicle for the purposes of the test is fully covered by a valid policy of insurance which satisfies the requirements of the relevant legislation.

- I normally live/have lived in the UK for at least 185 days in the last 12 months (except taxi/private hire). See note 30.

✗ _____

S ☐   D/C ☐

Application Ref. ☐☐☐☐☐☐☐☐

Date ☐☐☐☐☐☐   Time ☐☐☐☐   Dr./No. ☐☐☐☐☐☐

DTC Code / Authority ☐☐☐☐☐   Reg. No. ☐☐☐☐☐☐

Examiner   Staff / Ref. No. ☐☐☐☐☐☐

	Auto	Ext
Cat. Type ☐☐☐☐	☐	☐

1 ☐ 2 ☐ 3 ☐ 4 ☐ 5 ☐ 6 ☐ 7 ☐ 8 ☐ 9 ☐ 0 ☐ V ☐

ADI / Reg ☐☐☐☐☐☐   ADI Cert. No. ☐☐☐☐☐☐   Sup ☐   ADI ☐   Int ☐   Other ☐   C ☐

	Total	S	D
1a Eyesight			☐
1b H/Code / Safety	☐	☐	☐
2 Controlled Stop promptness	☐	☐	☐
control	☐	☐	☐
3 Reverse / Left Reverse with trailer control	☐	☐	☐
observation	☐	☐	☐
4 Reverse/ Right control	☐	☐	☐
observation	☐	☐	☐
5 Reverse Park control	☐	☐	☐
R ☐ C ☐ obs.	☐	☐	☐
6 Turn in road control	☐	☐	☐
observation	☐	☐	☐
7 Vehicle checks	☐	☐	☐
8 Taxi manoeuvre control	☐	☐	☐
observation	☐	☐	☐
9 Taxi wheelchair			☐
10 Uncouple / recouple		☐	☐
11 Precautions		☐	☐
12 Control accelerator	☐	☐	☐
clutch	☐	☐	☐
gears	☐	☐	☐
footbrake	☐	☐	☐
parking brake / MC front brake	☐	☐	☐
steering	☐	☐	☐
balance M/C	☐	☐	☐
LGV / PCV gear exercise	☐	☐	☐
PCV door exercise	☐	☐	☐

	Total	S	D
13 Move off safety	☐	☐	☐
control	☐	☐	☐
14 Use of mirrors- M/C rear obs. signalling	☐	☐	☐
change direction	☐	☐	☐
change speed	☐	☐	☐
15 Signals necessary	☐	☐	☐
correctly	☐	☐	☐
timed	☐	☐	☐
16 Clearance / obstructions	☐	☐	☐
17 Response to signs / signals traffic signs	☐	☐	☐
road markings	☐	☐	☐
traffic lights	☐	☐	☐
traffic controllers	☐	☐	☐
other road users	☐	☐	☐
18 Use of speed	☐	☐	☐
19 Following distance	☐	☐	☐
20 Progress appropriate speed	☐	☐	☐
undue hesitation	☐	☐	☐
21 Junctions approach speed	☐	☐	☐
observation	☐	☐	☐
turning right	☐	☐	☐
turning left	☐	☐	☐
cutting corners	☐	☐	☐
22 Judgement overtaking	☐	☐	☐
meeting	☐	☐	☐
crossing	☐	☐	☐

	Total	S	D
23 Positioning normal driving	☐	☐	☐
lane discipline	☐	☐	☐
24 Pedestrian crossings	☐	☐	☐
25 Position / normal stops	☐	☐	☐
26 Awareness / planning	☐	☐	☐
27 Ancillary controls	☐	☐	☐
28 Eco Safe Driving	☐	☐	☐
29 Spare 1	☐	☐	☐
30 Spare 2	☐	☐	☐
31 Spare 3	☐	☐	☐
32 Spare 4	☐	☐	☐
33 Wheelchair Pass ☐ Fail ☐			

Pass	Fail	None	Total Faults	Route No.
☐	☐	☐	☐☐	☐☐

ETA V ☐ P ☐   D255 ☐

Survey A ☐ B ☐ C ☐ D ☐
E ☐ F ☐ G ☐ H ☐

Debrief ☐   Activity Code ☐

I acknowledge receipt of Pass Certificate Number: Licence rec'd
☐☐☐☐☐☐☐☐   Yes ✗

Wheelchair Cert. No: COA ✗
☐☐☐☐☐☐☐☐   No ✗

There has been no change to my health; see note 29 overleaf.

✗ _____

Guidance Notes

DL25C Rev.

More detailed advice about the test requirements and the items marked for your attention overleaf are given in "The Driving Test Report Explained".

Further information may also be obtained from the relevant publication from the series of OFFICIAL driving books and other media products from DSA for all drivers and motorcyclists, including drivers of goods vehicles, buses and coaches, tractors and specialist vehicles.

These publications can be purchased from all good book shops or by visiting www.dsa.gov.uk

Explanatory Markings

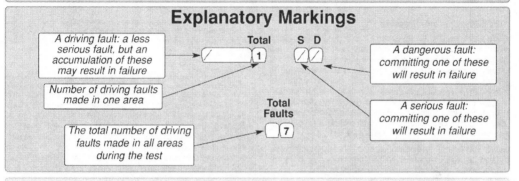

A driving fault: a less serious fault, but an accumulation of these may result in failure

Number of driving faults made in one area

The total number of driving faults made in all areas during the test

Total   S   D

Total Faults

A dangerous fault: committing one of these will result in failure

A serious fault: committing one of these will result in failure

The result of your test is marked overleaf, the following statement only applies if your result is marked as a fail.

Statement of Failure to Pass Practical Test – Test of Competence to Drive
Road Traffic Act 1988

This candidate named herein has been examined and has failed to pass the practical test / test of competence to drive prescribed under the Road Traffic Act 1988 (and for the purposes of Section 36 of the Road Traffic Offenders Act 1988 if an extended test).

Candidates are assessed against the items listed overleaf in deciding whether they are competent to drive. Items needing special attention are marked. You should study these along with the Guidance Notes above, and the 'Driving Test Report Explained' leaflet given to you by the examiner.

Unsuccessful candidates (dependent on category of test taken) may be required to wait a minimum period before taking a further test in a vehicle of the same category.

Appeals

If you consider that your test was not properly conducted in accordance with the relevant Regulations, you may apply to a Magistrate's Court acting for the Petty Sessions Area in which you reside (in Scotland to the Sheriff within whose jurisdiction you reside) which (who) has the power to determine this point. If you reside in England or Wales you have six months from the issue of this Statement of Failure in which to appeal, and if you reside in Scotland, 21 days. If the Court finds that the test was not properly conducted it may order a refund of the fee and authorise you to undergo a further test forthwith (see Road Traffic Act 1988 Section 90, for ADI qualifying tests see section 133).

You should note that your right to appeal to the Court under Section 90 or 133 are strictly limited to the question of whether the test was properly conducted in accordance with the relevant Regulations. **The examiner's decision and test result cannot be altered.**
Before you consider making any appeal you may wish to seek legal advice.

You can find details of our service standards and complaints procedures in our 'Customer Service: A guide to our service standards' leaflet, which is available from all our offices and test centres.

Data Protection and the use of your Personal Data

The Driving Test Report Explained

DL25D
04 / 07 T

1(a) Eyesight Test

At the start of the test the examiner asked you to read a vehicle registration number. If you required glasses or contact lenses, you must wear them whenever you drive. If you had problems with the eyesight test, perhaps you should consider consulting an optician.

1(b) Highway Code / Safety

If you didn't need to take a separate theory test, for example to obtain a licence for a tractor or other specialist vehicle, you will have been asked questions on the Highway Code and other related motoring matters. You will have also been asked to identify some traffic signs. If you had difficulty with these questions make sure that you study properly by reading as wide a range of publications as you can to increase your understanding. If you have already passed a theory test you will not have been asked Highway Code questions at the practical test stage; but you should still have a thorough knowledge of it.

Safety questions (if applicable) – you should know the location of, and be able to operate, safety components such as fire extinguisher, fuel cut-off switch and emergency door.

2 Controlled stop

You will need to be able to display a high level of skill in bringing your vehicle to a stop, safely, promptly and under full control avoiding locking the wheels. Remember that in wet weather it can take twice as long to stop safely.

3, 4 and 5 Reverse exercises

You will need to display the ability to control the vehicle safely whilst reversing to the left, right, when parking on the road or into a parking bay. You must take good effective all round observation throughout the manoeuvre and show consideration to other road users.

6 Turn in the road

You will need to display the low speed control and observation skills necessary to carry out this exercise safely with due regard for other road users and pedestrians.

7 Vehicle Checks

You will need to display to the examiner a basic knowledge of the fundamental safety checks applicable to your vehicle. For example safe fluid levels, lighting and tyre checks.

8 Taxi manoeuvre

You must be able to display the ability to turn your car around by whatever means available, making sure you take effective, all round observation showing consideration to other road users and pedestrians. You should control your vehicle smoothly making proper use of the clutch, accelerator, brakes and steering. You should not use a driveway or allow your vehicle to mount the pavement as this could damage your vehicle.

9 Taxi wheelchair

You should be able to securely erect wheelchair ramps, safely install the wheelchair and an imaginary wheelchair occupant into your vehicle, ensure the wheelchair and occupant are secured in readiness for the journey and reverse the entire process.

10 Vehicle and trailer combinations. Uncoupling / recoupling

You will need to demonstrate the skills necessary when uncoupling and recoupling your vehicle, driving the towing vehicle to a designated position prior to recoupling safely.

11 Precautions

Before you start the engine make sure that you are comfortably seated and all controls can be safely operated.

12 Control

This section covers, where appropriate, the safe and controlled use of accelerator, clutch, gears, footbrake, parking brake, and steering. Additional specific control elements apply to the drivers of different vehicle categories. Always try and use the vehicle controls as smoothly as possible. This means less wear and tear on your vehicle and a smoother ride for your passengers. Make proper use of your accelerator and clutch to make a smooth start. Always depress the clutch just before you stop. Select the correct gear to match the road and traffic conditions. Change gear in good time but not too soon before a hazard. Do not allow the vehicle to coast by running on in neutral or with the clutch depressed. There should be no need to look down at the gear lever when changing gear. Use the footbrake smoothly and progressively. Brake in plenty of time for any hazard. Make full use of the parking brake whenever it would help you to prevent the vehicle rolling backwards or forwards, and if you are parking. Steer the vehicle as smoothly as possible. Avoid harsh steering, or steering too early or too late as it may cause you to hit the kerb or swing out towards another road user. If you are riding a motorcycle slowly, maintain a straight line and do not allow the machine to wobble towards other vehicles.

13 Move off

You will need to demonstrate your ability to move off smoothly and safely on the level, on a gradient and at an angle taking the correct precautionary observations.

14 Use of mirrors – Rear observations

Use all the mirrors fitted to your vehicle safely and effectively. You must always check carefully before signalling, changing direction or changing speed. Use the Mirrors Signal Manoeuvre (MSM) routine effectively.

15 Signals

You must signal clearly to let others know what you intend to do. You should only use the signals shown in the Highway Code if it would help other road users (including pedestrians). Always signal in good time and ensure that the signal has been cancelled after the manoeuvre has been completed. Do not beckon to pedestrians to cross the road.

16 Clearance to obstructions

Allow plenty of room to pass stationary vehicles, obstructions and be prepared to slow down or stop. A door may open, a child may run out or a vehicle may pull out without warning.

The Driving Test Report Explained

DL25D Rev.

17 Response to signs/signals

You should understand and be able to react to all traffic signs and road markings. You must act correctly at traffic lights, and check that the road is clear before proceeding when the green light shows. Obey signals given by police officers, traffic wardens and school crossing patrols. Look out for signals given by other road users, including people in charge of animals, and be ready to act accordingly.

18 Use of speed

You should make safe, reasonable progress along the road bearing in mind the road, traffic and weather conditions and the road signs and speed limits. Make sure that you can stop safely, well within the distance you can see to be clear. Do not speed. Remember, as a new driver, your licence will be revoked if you accrue six or more penalty points during the first two years, and you will have to retake and pass both theory and practical tests.

19 Following distance

Always keep a safe distance between yourself and other vehicles. Remember, on wet or slippery roads it takes much longer to stop. When you stop in traffic queues leave sufficient space to pull out if the vehicle in front has problems.

20 Maintain progress

In order to pass your test you must show that you can drive at a realistic speed appropriate to the road and traffic conditions. You should approach all hazards at a safe, controlled speed, without being over cautious or interfering with the progress of other traffic. Always be ready to move away from junctions as soon as it is safe and correct to do so. Driving excessively slowly can create dangers for yourself and other drivers.

21 Junctions (including Roundabouts)

You should be able to judge the correct speed of approach so that you can enter a junction safely and stop if necessary. Position your vehicle correctly. Use the correct lane. If you are turning right, keep as near to the centre of the road as is safe. Avoid cutting the corner when turning right. If turning left, keep over to the left and do not swing out. Watch out for cyclists and motorcyclists coming up on your left and pedestrians who are crossing. You must take effective observation before moving into a junction and make sure it is safe before proceeding.

22 Judgement

Only overtake when it is safe to do so. Allow enough room when you are overtaking another vehicle. Cyclists and motorcyclists need as much space as other vehicles, they can wobble or swerve suddenly. Do not cut in too quickly after overtaking. Take care when the width of the road is restricted or when the road narrows. If there is an obstruction on your side or not enough room for two vehicles to pass safely, be prepared to wait and let the approaching vehicles through. When you turn right across the path of an approaching vehicle, make sure you can do so safely. Other vehicles should not have to stop, slow down or swerve to allow you to complete your turn.

23 Positioning

You should position the vehicle sensibly, normally well to the left. Keep clear of parked vehicles and position correctly for the direction that you intend to take. Where lanes are marked, keep to the middle of the lane and avoid straddling lane markings. Do not change lanes unnecessarily.

24 Pedestrian Crossings

You should be able to recognise the different types of pedestrian crossing and show courtesy and consideration towards pedestrians. At all crossings you should slow down and stop if there is anyone on the crossing. At zebra crossings you should slow down and be prepared to stop if there is anyone waiting to cross. Give way to any pedestrians on a pelican crossing when the amber lights are flashing. You should give way to cyclists as well as pedestrians on a toucan crossing and act correctly at puffin crossings.

25 Position / Normal stops

Choose a safe, legal and convenient place to stop, close to the edge of the road, where you will not obstruct the road and create a hazard. You should know how and where to stop without causing danger to other road users.

26 Awareness / Planning

You must be aware of other road users at all times. You should always think and plan ahead so you can judge what other road users are going to do, predict how their actions will affect you and react in good time. Take particular care to consider the actions of the more vulnerable groups of road users such as pedestrians, cyclists, motorcyclists and horse riders. Anticipate road and traffic conditions, and act in good time, rather than reacting to them at the last moment.

27 Ancillary controls

You should understand the function of all the controls and switches, especially those that have a bearing on road safety. These include indicators, lights, windscreen wipers, demisters and heaters. You should be able to find these controls and operate them correctly when necessary, without looking down.

28 Eco Safe Driving (if applicable)

Driving skills should demonstrate recognition of the principles of Eco Safe Driving, including appropriate use of the vehicle controls (Currently only applicable to certain categories of test).

29 Health Declaration

You must declare any change to your health status since you last applied for a licence. It is a criminal offence for you (or anyone else) to make a false statement in order for you to obtain a driving licence, and can lead to prosecution.

30 Residence

Normal residence means the place where you normally live and have personal or occupational ties. However, if you have moved to the UK from another European Country or European Economic Area (EC/EEA), you should not take a driving test or obtain a first full licence unless you have lived here for 185 days in the last 12 months and are still living here at the time of your licence application. You may be asked to provide evidence of this.

Manage your booking online at
www.direct.gov.uk/drivingtest

how2become

APPENDIX 4

THE CAUSES OF ROAD TRAFFIC COLLISIONS

The first fatal traffic collision in Britain was on 17 August 1896, in Crystal Palace, South East London, where a pedestrian, Bridget Driscoll was knocked down and killed by a car. Barely more than a couple of years later, the next collision involved the car's occupants being killed. On 23 February 1899, in Harrow on the Hill in North West London, the driver was attempting to turn a corner at over 25mph when one of the car's rear wheels collapsed and the vehicle hit a brick wall. The occupants were thrown out and the driver and front seat passenger killed. A roadside plaque records this incident and the newspapers at the time expressed hope that this terrible road accident would "convince drivers to take greater care and keep their speed down".

Nowadays, to establish the causes of road traffic collisions that are reported to the police, a very detailed form is completed. This document is known as the STATS19. The data from this record is accumulated electronically and yearly records are published in the 'GB Road Casualty Report'.

Human error is the main factor in 95% of road traffic collisions. Drivers are likely to blame other road users, including other drivers or the road conditions, or a mechanical failure. The report is very objective and presents the statistics in a very detailed way.

The report does indicate that Britain does have one of the best road safety records in Europe and the world, with a fall of fatalities to 1,901 in 2011 from

around 5,500 in the mid-1980s. The detail in this report is considerable and it is possible to present the information in different ways; however one feature that does remain constant is that driver error is the most common cause of road traffic collisions.

While there is some overlap in the information presented, the most common error identified is speeding. Around 430 people every year are killed in crashes in which someone is driving too fast for the conditions and possibly exceeding the speed limit. Driver inexperience is also a big factor. The number of people killed in crashes yearly, involving car drivers aged 17 to 24 years includes 150 young drivers, 90 passengers and more than 180 other road users.

300 deaths a year involve someone being "careless, reckless or in a hurry" along with a further 125 that involve "aggressive driving". 40% of road crashes involve someone who "failed to look properly". One third of fatal crashes involved "loss of control" of a vehicle. One in five crashes involve a road user failing to judge another person's path or speed.

Around 300 lives each year could be saved if everyone, including passengers, always wore their seat belt and around 250 people die a year in crashes in which someone was over the legal drink drive limit. This includes other road users and not just drunk drivers.

Discussion with instructors and other road safety experts are likely to identify the factors that contribute towards human error are:

- Inappropriate speed for the conditions.
- Driving too close.
- Poor hazard perception.
- Inexperience.

Drivers who are involved in collisions will recognise these factors, but include in their perception of what caused the collision other factors including poor health; distractions; stress and fatigue. As professional instructors, the technical and statistical information is important to us, however so are the lifestyle and journey issues that are covered in the European GDE Matrix (Chapter 9 of this Guide).

Young drivers, predominantly male, tend to crash at higher speeds than older drivers and late at night, or in the early morning. As new drivers, their skills are not fully automated and the following factors do aggravate the issue:

- Use of alcohol and/or the growing problem of drugs, both causing impairment).

- Distractions such as peer pressure and mobile phones

- Stress (Time pressures and life changing events – for instance: teen problems: moving home, relationships and love)

- Fatigue (Time of day/night)

In Chapter 8 we have put forward that driving instructors are in a key position to influence the next generation of drivers. Communicating the "safe driving for life message" is important to improving driving standards.

APPENDIX 5
NEW DRIVERS ACT 1995

This Act became effective in 1997. When learners pass the driving test, the New Drivers Act means that they are "on probation" for two years. If they reach six or more penalty points in that time, they'll lose their licence and will have to apply and pay for a new provisional licence. This means that they become learner drivers again.

Some learners get points on their provisional licences before passing their tests. These points last for three years and will count under the New Drivers Act. If they reach six points before they've taken their tests, the provisional licence isn't taken away, but if they get any more points within two years of passing their test, they will lose their licence.

Statistics indicate that 77% of revocations were males 25 and under; and 35% were males under 20. The Department for Transport identified that DVLA records suggest that half of all revocations are linked to driving uninsured (for which the penalty includes six points) and about a quarter for speeding offences.

Every week, about 300 new drivers lose their licences through this Act. An issue of serious concern is that only about half of the drivers who have had their licence revoked under the Act have recovered their full licence by passing both their theory and practical driving tests again. The maximum penalty for driving while disqualified is 6 months' imprisonment or a Level 5 fine (£5000).

Around half the drivers convicted for this offence each year are sent to prison.

The role of the driving instructor is to make sure that learners are fully aware of the driving offences and penalties given in the current edition of the 'Highway Code' (Page 126).

APPENDIX 6

IMPROVING THE STANDARD OF DRIVING INSTRUCTION

Prior to the voluntary Register of Approved Driving Instructors (ADI) being introduced in October 1964 the standards were set by the RAC through their Register of Instructors. In the first year, over 3000 instructors joined the government scheme by qualifying, claiming the new title of "Ministry of Transport Approved Driving Instructor".

In October 1970 the scheme became compulsory, requiring anyone who wished to give paid instruction in cars, to qualify and have their name entered into the Register by law. There have been various changes to its structure and the qualifying process over the years and Chapter 10 of this Guide describes the current examination and licensing system for driving instructors.

Users of this Guide need to be aware that this system is under review and changes to modernise driver training may come into effect within the next couple of years.

The qualifying process has been looked at with proposals to allow the industry to both train and enter successful instructors onto the Register. DSA would have a quality assurance role by providing a Check Test soon after the qualification has been achieved. Under continued consideration is replacement of the current 'trainee driving instructor licence' scheme with a full supervision process. A long standing promise to introduce mandatory

Continuing Professional Development (CPD) has been shelved recently, despite popularity within the driving school industry and with other road safety consultative organisations.

A new occupational standard for learning to drive has been published. This has been trademarked by DSA as the 'National Driver / Rider Training Standard' (NDRTS). As with NVQs, the criteria includes knowledge and understanding, combined with practical skills.

This standard sets out a comprehensive syllabus for learning to drive, from which changes may be derived for the current ADI examination. This may possibly pave a way as to introduce a new vocational instructor qualification to replace the existing arrangements.

Other driver training improvements that have been on the table for a long time include:

1. Invigorating the 'Pass Plus' scheme.

2. Allowing learners accompanied by ADIs to drive on motorways.

To keep up to date on the proposals, join one or more of the industry trade associations. Their contact details are published in this guide.

APPENDIX 7
USEFUL CONTACTS

This is a list of the organisations that are mostly likely to be able to assist you in various ways in your new career as a driving instructor. Although it is not an exclusive list it does include most of the key players in this industry.

We recommend that for details of commercial organisations and suppliers, that you contact one or more of the driving school associations and ask them to send you a complimentary copy of their latest magazine. You will also find helpful information on the association websites.

1. DRIVING STANDARDS AGENCY (DSA)

DSA is one of the Executive Agencies within the Department for Transport. It promotes road safety through setting standards for drivers, riders and trainers, testing drivers and riders fairly and efficiently, maintaining the registers of Approved Driving Instructors; Large Goods Vehicle Instructors; Fleet Trainers; Driving Instructor Trainers and Post-Test Motorcycle Trainers; supervising Compulsory Basic Training (CBT) for learner motorcyclists and driver education and the provision of learning resources.

> Driving Standards Agency
> The Axis Building
> 112 Upper Parliament Street
> Nottingham, NG1 8LP
>
> T: 0300 200 1122
> E: adireg@dsa.gsi.gov.uk
> W: www.gov.uk
> Magazine: Despatch ezine

2. MOTOR SCHOOLS ASSOCIATION (MSA)

The Motor Schools Association of Great Britain (MSA) was formed on March 31, 1935, just before the driving test was introduced. The association's principal aims, then as now, are to keep members informed of any matters of interest to them, to represent the views of members to Government, its departments and agencies, to provide services that will be of benefit to members and to set standards of professional and ethical behaviour for teachers of driving.

> Motor Schools Association
> 101 Wellington Road North, Stockport
> Cheshire, SK4 2LP
>
> T: 0161 429 9669
> E: mail@msagb.co.uk
> W: www.msagb.com
> Magazine: Newslink

3. DRIVING INSTRUCTORS ASSOCIATION (DIA)

The DIA is the largest association for professional driving instructors in the UK. It has consultative status with the DSA and has representation in both Parliament and in Europe. DIA members automatically qualify for £10m Public Liability and £5m Professional Indemnity (PL/PI) cover.

Driving Instructors' Association
Leon House
233 High Street,
Croydon, CR0 9XT

T: 020 8686 8010
E: dia@driving.org
W: www.driving.org
Magazine: Driving Instructor

4. APPROVED DRIVING INSTRUCTORS NATIONAL JOINT COUNCIL (ADINJC)

The ADINJC is the fastest growing national driving instructor association in the UK. Known as "the Association of Associations", driving instructors who are not in a local driving instructor association can join the Driving Instructor Group (DIG) as individual members. ADINJC is run by working ADIs on a voluntary basis and provides support, advice and representation to fellow ADIs.

Approved Driving Instructors National Joint Council (ADINJC)
47 Sweetmans Road
Shaftesbury, SP7 8EH

T: 01747 855091
E: adinjc_liaisonofficer@hotmail.co.uk
W: www.adinjc.org.uk

5. INSTITUTE OF MASTER TUTORS OF DRIVING (IMTD)

The IMTD is a small, but well respected, 'behind the scenes' organisation that has as its members some of the most experienced, highly qualified and successful road safety practitioners and Approved Driving Instructors in the UK and Ireland. IMTD is a not-for-profit organisation that keeps its members informed about the latest developments and technology in road safety and driver instruction.

Institute of Master Tutors of Driving (IMTD)
85 Highbank Drive
Garston
Liverpool, L19 5PG

T: 0151 280 4248
E: houseofhiggins@btinternet.com
W: www.imtd.org.uk

6. ASSOCIATION OF INDUSTRIAL ROAD SAFETY OFFICERS (AIRSO)

AIRSO is an independent membership organisation working in the interests of road safety, highly respected in the field within the public, private and voluntary sectors. Members represent a wide cross-section, including commercial transport, fleet management, driver training, independent and local government road safety organisations, the armed services, the emergency services and enforcement agencies. Membership of AIRSO is open to any person whose work is in any way connected with the promotion of road safety.

Association of Industrial Road Safety Officers (AIRSO)
68 The Boulevard
Worthing
West Sussex, BN13 1LA

T: 01903 506095
E: info@airso.org.uk
W: www.airso.org.uk

7. PEOPLE 1ST (PCV/HOSPITALITY/TRAVEL/TOURISM)

People 1st is one of 24 Sector Skills Councils recognised by the government. It is an industry-focused body established to support the development of skills and training. It is responsible for setting the National Occupational Standards for NVQs including those relevant to the passenger transport industry.

People 1st
2nd Floor, Armstrong House
38 Market Square
Uxbridge, UB8 1LH

T: 01895 817000
E: welcome@people1stmail.co.uk
W: www.people1st.co.uk

8. SKILLS FOR LOGISTICS (LGV/HGV)

Skills for Logistics is the Sector Skills Council with responsibility for skill and productivity development within the UK's freight logistics industries. It provides the basis for career apprenticeships for goods drivers and transport staff working within the haulage industry.

Skills for Logistics
12 Warren Yard
Warren Farm Office Village
Milton Keynes, MK12 5NW

T: 01908 313360
E: info@skillsforlogistics.org
W: www.skillsforlogistics.org

9. THE INSTITUTE OF ADVANCED MOTORISTS (IAM)

The IAM is a road safety charity based in Chiswick, West London. The organisation has more than two hundred voluntary affiliated groups around the country. Individual members of these groups have taken and passed the advanced test and often make themselves available to help others do the same.

Institute of Advanced Motorists
510 Chiswick High Road
London, W4 5RG
T: 020 8996 9600
E: info@iam.org.uk
W: www.iam.org.uk
Magazine: Advanced Driving

10. ROYAL SOCIETY FOR THE PREVENTION OF ACCIDENTS (ROSPA)

RoSPA's Advanced Drivers' and Riders' Association is a charity based in Birmingham. They have a network of over 50 local groups around the UK. These groups have trained and experienced tutors willing to offer free advice, assessments and support to help drivers and motorcyclists prepare for their Advanced Driving/Motorcycling test.

> Royal Society for the Prevention of Accidents
> 28 Calthorpe House
> Edgbaston
> Birmingham, B15 1RP

> T: 0121 248 2000
> E: help@rospa.com
> W: www.rospa.com
> Magazine: Care on the Road

11. THE ADI FEDERATION

Set up in 1996 to help and assist the individual professional ADI, the ADI Federation is a non-profit making association. It works closely with and alongside the DSA and is more able to get problems sorted in minimum time, leaving our members to get on with what they do best – teaching people driving skills and good practice on the roads.

> The ADI Federation Ltd
> Kingsmith House
> 63a Marshalls Road
> Raunds, Northants NN9 6EY

> T: 01933-461821
> E: info@theadifederation.org.uk
> W: www.theadifederation.org.uk

12. THE DIDU ASSOCIATION – DELIVERING INFORMATION DEVELOPING UNDERSTANDING

DIDU is an association of driving instructors. It is run by driving instructors, for driving instructors. Membership is open to all ADIs and PDIs. It offers CPD courses, free online CPD, local and national representation, along with a busy internet forum.

DIDU
PO Box 165
Northallerton, DL6 2WX

T: 01609 881034
E: didu@arwcsw.com
W: www.didu.co.uk
Magazine: Empower

13. THE DRIVING INSTRUCTORS SCOTTISH COUNCIL (DISC)

The Driving Instructors Scottish Council is a body of representatives of most of the ADIs in Scotland, giving a voice to almost two-thirds of the country's instructors. It has consultative status with the DSA and is in regular contact with its officials, therefore being able to instantly liaise on any subject connected with road safety and the well-being of instructors.

The Driving Instructors Scottish Council (DISC)
6 Auldgavel Place
Strathaven, ML10 6DE

T: 01357 522420
E: j@jmiller9.wanadoo.co.uk
W: www.d-i-s-c.org.uk

14. THE MOTOR CYCLE INDUSTRY TRAINERS ASSOCIATION

1 Rye Hill Office Park
Birmingham Road
Allesley, Coventry CV5 9AB

T: 02476 408 032
E: enquiries@mcita.co.uk
W: www.mcita.co.uk

15. QUEEN ELIZABETH FOUNDATION (QEF)

The origins of QEF can be traced back as far as 1932. Today it is a leading disability charity working with people that have physical and learning disabilities, or acquired brain injuries, to help them gain new skills and increase independence for life.

QEF Mobility Services
Carshalton
Surrey, SM5 4NR

T: 01372 841100
E: mobility@qef.org.uk
W: www.qef.org.uk

16. THE NATIONAL TRAILER & TOWING ASSOCIATION (NTTA)

The NTTA was founded in 1975 and sets the standards for the towing industry today. They have a specialist driving school listing on their website and provide expert advice on the skills and expertise necessary for drivers to tow trailers, including caravans and horse boxes safely.

NTTA
Carriage Court
Welbeck
Worksop, S80 3LR

T: 01909 512555
W: www.ntta.co.uk

APPENDIX 8
OTHER RECOMMENDED PUBLICATIONS

i.   The Highway Code – Available free online.

ii. Know Your Traffic Signs – Available free online.

iii. Your Road to Becoming a Driving Instructor (ADI 14) – available free online.

iv. Casualty Report 2011 (Government Statistical Source) – available free online.

v.   Driving – The Essential Skills. Published by The Stationery Office. Available online for payment.

vi. The Driving Instructor's Handbook   John Miller & Margaret Stacey – Book available as a purchase from Amazon and good bookshops.

APPENDIX 9

GLOSSARY OF TERMS

AA	Automobile Association
ABS	Anti-Lock Braking System
ADI	Approved Driving Instructor (Car)
ADINJC	ADI Joint Council
AIRSO	Association of Industrial Road Safety Officers
ATB	AApproved Training Body (Motorcycle)
BTEC	Business Technical & Education Council (Awarding body – Edexcel)
CBT	Compulsory Basic Training (Motorcycles)
CPD	Continuing Professional Development
DAS	Direct Access Scheme (Motorcycles)
dCPC	Driver Certificate of Professional Competence
DIA	Driving Instructors Association
DSA	Driving Standards Agency
ESP	Electronic Stability Programme

HGV	Heavy Goods Vehicle
IAM	Institute of Advanced Motorists
ITN	Identify Training Needs
LGV	Large Goods Vehicle
MiDAS	Minibus Driver Assessment Scheme
MSA	Motor Schools Association
NDRTS	National Driver/Rider Training Standard
NSL	National Speed Limit
NVQ	National Vocational Qualification
ORDIT	Official Register of Driving Instructor Training
PDI	Potential Driving Instructor
PCV	Passenger Carrying Vehicle
PST	Pre-Set Test (ADI Examination)
Q&A	'Question and Answer' technique
RoSPA	Royal Society for the Prevention of Accidents
RPM	(Engine) Revs Per Minute
RPMT	Register of Post-test Motorcycle Trainers

how2become

Visit www.how2become.co.uk for more
career and testing titles:

- How to pass any career selection process
- How to pass any job interview
- How to pass psychometric tests
- 1-day intensive training courses

www.how2become.co.uk